up-close

A *Spiritual Life Notebook* to Fuel Your
Growth in Christ

Up-Close: A Spiritual Life Notebook to Fuel Your Growth in Christ

© 2024, 2017, 2013, 2009 by Forge. All rights reserved.

© 1981 by Dwight Robertson.

Published by Forge, 14485 East Evans Avenue,

Denver, Colorado 80014

ISBN 978-1-960455-03-1 (paperback)

Edited by Charlie Marq and Emily Adams.

Cover and layout by Stephanie Andersson.

contents

up-close
a spiritual life notebook to fuel your growth in christ

my spiritual life notebook
60-day supply of pages

a note from the spiritual life notebook creator

Early in my walk with God, I came into contact with a small group of Christians who seemed different from most of the other Christians I knew. They were excited about Jesus and they talked about Him as if they *really* knew Him—deeply and intimately.

And they were hungry to know Him more.

They shared their fresh insights from reading His Word. They quoted Scripture from memory. Their prayer lives seemed vibrant and consistent. They spoke to God and He spoke to them—as if they were close friends who communicated often.

They experienced a deep relationship with God—and they were continually going deeper!

More and more, their passion for God—and their obvious joy in knowing Him—created in me a "holy disturbance." "Holy" because it brought me into God's presence. A "disturbance" because it stirred a new hunger inside of me for more of God.

I was eager to leave my shallow walk behind. I wanted what they had. I wanted to know God like them. I wanted to go deeper into His Word and discover Him more fully, just like them.

But I wasn't sure how.

For the next few months, I pursued God with more energy than ever before. I fervently prayed and read the Bible like I was told, but I still wasn't really growing like I wanted. Something was missing.

That's when I discovered an insight into spiritual growth that has helped me as much as anything else in my spiritual journey. It wasn't profound or complex. In fact, it was really very simple. I just pulled out a pen and paper and began writing down everything God was speaking to me.

When He spoke to me during prayer, I wrote it down. When He spoke to me through His Word, I wrote it down. When He spoke to me through a pastor's message or through conversations with friends, I wrote it down.

Then, I consistently re-read and reflected on my previous entries.

I was amazed to discover that God spoke to me . . . a lot! I just hadn't recognized it or acted on what He said. But the more I wrote everything down, the more I recognized His voice and responded to it.

For years, whenever God spoke to me, I jotted it down on any leftover scraps of paper that were lying around. If I was in a restaurant, I used a napkin. At church, I used the back of a worship bulletin. But over time, the scraps of paper, napkins, and church bulletins began to pile up and created a disorganized mess!

Realizing I needed a better system for organizing my notes, I bought a simple, spiral-bound notebook. Into it, I recorded the different aspects of my spiritual life: prayer requests, journal entries, sermon notes, and Scriptures I was memorizing.

Within a few months I filled up several notebooks. Clearly, I was quickly outgrowing this system!

I needed something expandable—a system that could grow along with my spiritual life. So, I organized the different aspects of my walk with God into a three-ring binder. Then I added or deleted sections, adapting the notebook to whatever helped me grow deeper.

As the spiritual value (and benefits) of my notebook increased, I began creating them for others as well. Over and over, I witnessed people going deeper in their relationships with God, helped by their spiritual life notebook.

Amazingly, since the first version of Spiritual Life Notebook was created in 1981, tens of thousands of people have discovered—with me —that this is an invaluable tool for helping them grow deeper in their relationship with Jesus.

Now, as you walk with Jesus—for the first time or perhaps for the first time in a long time, I pray this guide will help you grow and mature in your relationship with Him, too.

For the King and the Kingdom,

Dwight Robertson
Spiritual Life Notebook Creator
Forge Founder & President

why a spiritual life notebook?

Train Tracks, Mighty Oaks, & Lifelong Companions

What do trains, trees, and soul mates all have in common? When it comes to knowing God and growing in your relationship with Him— quite a lot! Each of these metaphors represent ways of understanding what our daily life with God is about and how we go about growing and deepening our relationship with Him.

Take the train tracks for instance. Trains have destinations. They are a wonderful means to get places we want to go. A train without tracks, however, doesn't go far. Tracks guide the train all along the way to take us where we want to go. A daily life with God is a bit like train tracks. Our desired destination is to become more like Jesus and serve Him in His Kingdom— "to grow in wisdom and stature and favor with God and others" as Jesus did (Luke 2:52). Our daily rhythms, practices, and disciplines all serve as tracks to guide us toward that end.

Perhaps the metaphor of a tree may also be helpful. The oak tree is among the strongest trees on earth. Its roots are deep, it's branches sturdy, its foundation stout. Yet, these magnificent trees have humble beginnings as acorns (about the size of a grape), they fall to the ground, sink beneath earth's surface, and begin to germinate and grow. How does a little acorn become a mighty oak? God waters and grows it—day after day, year after year, decade by decade.

That's the way God grows us. We don't become mighty oaks (or anything else) on our own. We simply position ourselves to be watered and tended by God. He does the growing as we daily put ourselves in a posture to be grown and respond to whatever tilling He may be doing in our life. Little by little—through seasons of sun, wind, snow, and rain—God grows us into the *mighty oaks* He's always intended.

Or, maybe a growing love relationship paints a good picture for you. Consider the couple who's been married for sixty years, or kindred friendships like Jonathan and David or Ruth and Naomi from the Scriptures. Deep and abiding relationships just don't happen overnight. Time spent knowing one another, learning about each other, and experiencing life's trials as well as triumphs together makes for long-lasting, like-no-other, deep and abiding love.

As we spend our daily life *with* Jesus, our relationship with Him deepens and matures. We learn from Him, experience life with Him, enjoy His presence, and trust His loving leadership.

Whatever metaphor we use, a daily life with Jesus is about knowing Him (far beyond just knowing *about* Him) and growing deeper in our love and service with Him. This *Spiritual Life Notebook* is designed to help you daily become all that God intends and to experience all He desires as one He loves and who labors in His Kingdom.

Spiritual Practice: Who You Will Be, You Are Now Becoming

Great people and great things just don't appear one day. The Great Pyramids didn't just rise from the Egyptian sands one morning. "Rome," as the saying goes, "wasn't built in a day." Nor do people just suddenly arrive. Consider your favorite musician, athlete, billionaire, humanitarian, or relationship. He or she didn't just pop on the scene all put together and famous. Most likely, they spent years honing their craft, sweating the details, learning from mistakes, and doing what most every novice and amateur rolls their eyes at when hearing a coach or mentor say: "Practice, practice, practice!"

Becoming God's best version of yourself takes practice. Spiritual and emotional growth develop over time the same way that physical growth does. Consider babies learning to walk. Or adults working out. Whether at a gym or at home, any single workout routine doesn't suddenly make one fit. But, as one looks back over time, the day-by-day sweat begins to make sense and literally take shape as we measure ourselves—not by where we are, but by how far we've come.

Maybe you're reading this as a new believer. If so, welcome to God's Kingdom—it's the best decision you will ever make! The decision you've made is the start of the relationship God always meant for you. Note the word "start." Your new life with Jesus is just beginning. It's not an endpoint. No need to strive to become "the perfect Christian" (because here's a little secret, perfect Christians don't exist!).

Replace the word *perfect* with the word *practice* in your walk with Jesus, and you're well on your way to becoming more mature in your relationship with Him. So starting today, relax. Begin *practicing* getting up-close to God, *practicing* putting love into action, *practicing* sharing God's Good News with others—one moment, one encounter, one day at a time.

That's why we say, "Who you will be, you are now becoming." Your daily encounters with God now will not only equip you for the day and moments you're presently in, they will also become spiritual building blocks that will make you more and more the person God has always had in mind.

One of Jesus' closest followers, Paul, said it this way:

And I pray that you, being rooted and established in love, may have power, together with all the Lord's holy people, to grasp how wide and long and high and deep is the love of Christ, and to know this love that surpasses knowledge—that you may be filled to the measure of all the fullness of God.
- Ephesians 3:17-19

"The fullness of GOD," that's the goal! Not us *measuring up*, rather, being more and more *filled up* with the fullness of who God is and what He does! That's something that takes practice whether we're a brand new Christian or have been following Jesus for a while.

A quick note to those in *restart* mode. Perhaps you committed your life to Jesus a long time ago, and for a whole host of reasons, you feel like you've spent a lot of time trying to measure up instead of being filled up. If that's your story, please know two things. One, you're in the right place! And two, this is a "no shame" zone! Jesus isn't interested in a spiritual timetable. What He is interested in is your heart and willingness to live up-close to Him and develop daily rhythms of knowing, loving, enjoying, and serving Him.

Practicing Your Greatest Gift

"The greatest gift you can offer the world is your intimacy with God." That phrase is not only catchy, it's true! The closer we get relationally up-close to God, the better we will love and serve others as God does.

Getting up-close with God doesn't happen instantly. No more than a newly married couple has marriage all figured out after they get back from their honeymoon. Love and relationships take shape, get deeper (and more fulfilling!) as those who are in the relationship devote themselves to one another in up-close engagement. You might be tempted to think that love and relationships take shape and get deeper "over time." It would be a mistake to think that way. Time by itself does not deepen and mature relationships—intentional growth through knowing, understanding, and engaging does!

Your goal, then, is to daily engage the God who loves you—to know and understand Him, to daily "walk" (do life) with Him, enjoy Him, and to learn to recognize His voice and do what pleases Him.

That's what it means to have intimacy with God. And, getting up-close to God takes practice so that it becomes the daily rhythm of our life.

The more we practice a lifestyle of getting up-close to God, the more it becomes the driving habit and source of all we say, think, and do.

No Guessing Games: God Gives Us What We Need Relationally

God doesn't play guessing games with us. He doesn't say, "Figure out what pleases me, and if you guess right, I'll consider loving you." No, God says right up front, *"When you seek me with your whole heart, you will find me"* (Jeremiah 29:13, emphasis added). God doesn't hide from us. He not only makes Himself "easily found," He connects with us in ways that He knows we are uniquely wired in finding and knowing Him.

There are places God promises to meet us: in His Word, in prayer, in the company of other believers, in creation, etc. That is why developing a practice of encountering God in places He is sure to meet us makes sense and becomes so important. Practicing a rhythm of meeting God in these places opens our ears, eyes, heart, and mind to all kinds of other places, people, and situations God is alive in and at work. The more attentive we become in these known and familiar places, the more aware we become to God meeting us in ways unique to how we think, feel, process, and understand.

The psalm-writer, David, says knowing and experiencing God is as natural as a deer lapping up water in a cool stream on a hot day (Psalm 42:1). Connecting with God is in your DNA! It may take a little reacclimatizing, reviving, or awakening, but rest assured—you were made for this!

Don't Worry, You're Not Alone

Starting anything new can be intimidating, frustrating, and confusing. Beginning a life of getting daily up-close to God can certainly include all those things. It's easy to feel like "I'm not doing it right," or "I just don't understand how this works."

If that describes you, know that God is more delighted by your desire to get up-close to Him than He is any perfect performance or marked-off checklists you can muster. If you are authentically seeking after God and desiring with all your heart to please Him, you are getting it right!

As for the rest, plenty of good "helps" are available to you through Forge and other ministries that care deeply about people knowing and following Jesus. We highly encourage you to get connected to a local church, get involved in a small group of believers, and prayerfully consider a trusted spiritual mentor if available.

These connections, while often beneficial, are not always available. So, don't feel like you have to have them to know Jesus and serve Him. You don't. We're just encouraging you to take hold of the opportunities when God brings them to you. They often help us get further faster in knowing Jesus and maturing in our relationship with Him.

The Most Important Step: The First One

A 2,300 year old Chinese proverb by Laozi reads, "A journey of a thousand miles begins with a single step." It's true! Then another step, and another, and another. Mighty oaks, anticipated train destinations, and cherished relationships all begin small and continue to grow, find traction, and mature one day at a time—day, by day, by day. And you will find a rhythm of loving God and people too through the God-given, time-tested, catalysts for getting up-close to God in this guide. May His love grow *in* you and flow *through* you.

you do you

Training Wheels, Starter Kits, and Jesus

The goal of this notebook is to *guide* you toward maturity in Jesus Christ. Notice the emphasis on *guide*. While these practices are Biblical, tested over time, and contain places God Himself has promised to meet you—the aim of this guide is to get you up-close to Jesus, not make you a superstar at practicing religious things.

So consider this resource more like training wheels or a starter kit. The guide will get you going and give you some basic instructions to point you in the right direction (toward Jesus!). But we are also confident Jesus Himself will help shape your intimacy with Him in ways that fit you perfectly and will steadily guide you toward becoming all He desires.

Several Ways to Use This Guide—You Do You

Up-Close is designed to fit wherever you are in your daily practice of getting up-close to Jesus. If you are a brand new Christian and just getting started, we've got you covered. If you made a commitment to Jesus a while ago, and feel like you just haven't gained depth or traction in your relationship with Him, we've got you covered too. Or, even if you have been walking in a deep and fruitful relationship with Jesus for many years, there are likely still some approaches and tools here that can further equip you. *Up-Close* is written to be flexible and adaptable to wherever you are in your journey with Jesus and whatever best connects with your unique way of ordering your thoughts and engagements with God and others.

3 Basic Approaches

One-Stop Shop—If you are getting started for the first time, *Up-Close* will walk with you through a 60-day time period. The first half of the book will teach you how to engage daily rhythms and practices. The second half of the book contains everything you need to practice connecting with and encountering Jesus for 60 days. After you fill up all the pages in this notebook, additional blank Spiritual Life Notebook journal pages (formatted without the written guides and introductions to each section) are available through Forge.

B.Y.O.B. (Bring Your Own Bible, Journal, etc.)—If you already have a spiritual journal or notebook you like to use, this may be the approach for you. While we recommend you begin in this journal to get a feel for these spiritual growth practices, you may prefer to transition these concepts over to a journal or notebook of your own (especially once this notebook is full). If that sounds more like you, you can create, adapt, or copy the concepts and journal pages in this notebook to fill the pages of your own journal.

A Hybrid Approach—If you have other creative ways of recording and organizing your life and thoughts, incorporate them. If you use your phone to organize your daily life, perhaps a note app or filing system will work best for you. You might even check out the electronic Spiritual Life Notebook available through the Forge App

(TheForgeApp.com). Or, perhaps it will be a combination of things—like a journal to write in and your phone to organize prayer requests. Maybe you have several smaller notebooks for different categories that make sense to you.

Use or create whatever approach is simple and doable for you. Remember, the goal is to daily engage Jesus and serve His Kingdom—not become a spiritual life notebook superstar. Let the guide serve you, don't become a servant to the guide.

4 Solid Peers

Knowing the depths of God is like trying to personally snorkel every inch of the seven seas—it just isn't happening in the span of a lifetime! To this date in history, scientists and explorers have only discovered about 10% of all the oceans have and hold. Still, every encounter, every new discovery amazes us and leaves us in awe. Knowing God is a little like that. He is an ocean we will never fully conquer or master. Still, every encounter and discovery of Him leaves us amazed and wanting more.

Whether exploring the vast oceans or the vastness of God who made the oceans, it's easy to wonder how to get started and where to begin. Because God loves us so much, He doesn't keep us guessing or leave it all up to us to solve. God gives us ways to meet and know Him! This guide focuses on four of those ways.

Each of these ways of daily encountering God are like piers in the ocean. They give us a solid foundation and place to stand in seeing, experiencing, and engaging God.

The four piers in your Spiritual Life Notebook are:

1. **God's Word**—Knowing God through knowing what He has done, what He desires of you, what He is up to in His Kingdom, and how He made you to be a part.

2. **Prayer**—Up-close communication with God. An opportunity to praise and adore Him and to align yourself with what God is up to in the world, the lives of others, and your own life.

3. **Daily Reflection**—Evaluating where you have been, where you are, and where you are going.

4. **Kingdom Investment**—My life becoming a seed that falls into the ground and dies that it might sprout new life, bear fruit, multiply, and help others.

Notice that each of these have aspects of loving and knowing God and loving and knowing others. They are both what God does *in* us and what God does *through* us! They help mature a *heart on fire, life on purpose* lifestyle with God and others. As you daily engage God in these four areas, your relationship will continue to grow and mature.

Learn, Do, Repeat, Grow!

Getting up-close to God was never meant to be complicated. And we certainly don't want to make it that way! Here is the basic approach:

Learn. Read the material and instruction in this guide and learn all you can about the journey of knowing and maturing in your relationship with Jesus. Throughout this guide, you will also be introduced and invited to other resources (videos, books, links) to give you as much help as you want and need.

Do. Doing helps us to better understand and solidify the things we are learning. Don't just read about the forms and practices, do them! Each section has journal pages you can mark up, practice with, and use. Don't worry about "not doing it right." Right and wrong ways are not what this guide is about. So, write in the margins, highlight all over the place, and fill out the journal pages as you get to them. This guide has a whole section of journal pages to help you practice and experiment getting up-close with God. For now, practice using the journal pages as you come across them.

Repeat. Whether you use the *Spiritual Life Notebook: 60-Day Starter* in the back of this guide or B.Y.O.B. or hybrid approach, getting started and repeating these "holy habits" daily for 60 days is crucial. Repetition helps create rhythms and structures in our lives that take us where we want to go. Any successful athlete, student, musician, artist, or craftsman will tell you as much. So, start using your Spiritual Life Notebook immediately and commit to engaging God daily through it for 60 days.

Grow. You have read it already, now hear it again: The goal of this guide is not to make you a Spiritual Life Notebook superstar. It is to help you get started in getting up-close to God and maturing in your relationship with Him. So, soak in all you can. Learn as much as you can, wherever you can. Commit to God that you will be a lifelong student of all He wants to teach you and do in and through you.

Spiritual Life Notebook Journaling Tips

1. Write down God's words to you.

If remembering God and His work in our lives is important, then we should employ every available tool to prevent us from forgetting them. One of our greatest tools is simply writing down what He's teaching us.

The ideas and thoughts God speaks to you are more valuable than diamonds—treasures that are worth more than anything money can buy. Recording them is like hiding them in a safe place, where you can remember them, repeatedly return to them, and more fully integrate them into your heart and life.

God speaks in many different ways: his Word, your thoughts, circumstances, a pastor's message, a book, a friend . . . His means of communicating with us are endless. But what does it communicate to God if you don't value *His personal words to you* enough to record them so you can more fully meditate and act on them?

When you place yourself in a listening posture—with pen in hand—you embody a humble, hungry student who wants to learn from the Master Teacher—the one who knows all things. Why wouldn't you want to record the things He shares with you? They're the essence of abundant life!

2. Record your thoughts and feelings.

Most of us call this journaling. When we journal, we draw out the thoughts and feelings that reside deep within us. This spiritual discipline forces us to process, refine, and focus those thoughts and feelings in order to put them into words.

And that makes them real to us. But it also allows us to better express these thoughts and feelings with other intimate allies in our lives.

One way to journal is to write out your prayers. This enables you to identify the sources of stress, doubt, and pain in your life and bring them to God. As you write them down, you can release your emotions to God and ask Him to replace your burdens with joy and peace.

3. Review and reapply.

But writing everything down isn't enough. Our written records lose power over time unless we review and celebrate the past. We can reapply lessons and truths to our present—celebrating and perhaps even avoiding mistakes in the future. This is one of the greatest tools to remember what God has taught us.

Repetition helps us remember. Repetition helps us remember. Repetition helps us remember. You get the point.

4. Pass it on.

Rather than keep your growth to yourself, pass it on. God didn't bless you so you can hoard the blessings. He wants you to share them with others.

If He's taught you anything, He wants you to teach it to others. If he's ever strengthened you, He wants you to strengthen others. If He's comforted you, He wants you to comfort others. If He's blessed you with spiritual resources, He wants you to share them with others. Don't be a cup that only receives. Be a pipeline that gives as you receive.

Handholds and Free Climbing

If you have ever seen a picture of someone free-climbing the rock face of a mountain, it probably amazed you and made your hands sweat at the same time. How do they climb with such confidence when so many dangers surround them?

Intuitively, we know this must not be the climbers first climb. Their climbing expertise most likely began many years prior with someone showing them very simple handholds that would allow them to grow and excel in their climbing.

That's exactly what *Up-Close* is meant to do. The next several chapters are instructions on how to have good handholds in Prayer, God's Word, Daily Reflection, and Kingdom Investment.

We're confident that as you grasp hold of these handholds, your confidence will increase and you will grow and excel in your relationship with God in ways that continue to look like and resonate with you.

Consider *Up-Close* your basic instructor. God is the Expert. He will lead you to free-climbing mountain adventures far beyond any basic, manual instruction.

But climbing mountains does usually begin with learning handholds. And—this resource is full of all the getting up-close to God handholds you will need to get started.

So, follow the instructions, soak in the tips, learn the basics, utilize the journal pages, watch the linked videos, and practice getting up-close to God daily.

Your up-close adventure with God is a page-turn away!

up-close

A Spiritual Life Notebook to Fuel Your Growth
in Christ

up-close in god's word

. . .

engaging god's word as a lifestyle

If you have ever fallen in love (or desire to someday!), you will understand the statement, "When you love someone, you can't wait to know all about them!" You can't wait for the next conversation, letter, or connection. You look for every opportunity, nugget, or insight to know all you can about them. You want to discover who they are, what they like, and what will please them.

God's Word is a lot like that for us. It's a way God helps us know more about who He is, what He is like, what pleases Him, and what it looks like to join Him in loving others.

Spending time in God's Word is more than reading good stories and gaining some sound guidance for life. God's Word isn't about gaining more information *about* God. God's Word is an opportunity to *know* God Himself—up-close, personally, intimately. And as we engage God in His Word, His words, thoughts, heartbeat, and mission become ours. His words become a part of our everyday conversations. His wisdom influences our daily decisions. His agenda sets our priorities. His heart for others shapes our calendars. Reading and engaging God's Word isn't something we occasionally *do*, it's our daily source for knowing and loving God and others.

God's Word

The Bible is full of truth and life. It is a gift that paints a picture of who God really is and how much he loves us. It shows His mighty works, His mysterious ways, His timeless values, His amazing character, and the depths of His heart for those He created and loves.

That is why digging deep into the Bible is, along with prayer, one of the best ways to grow in Christ. It's one of our primary means of knowing God, more of who He is, and more about who we are in relationship to Him.

Spiritual Dynamite

While some people refer to the Bible as "the Good Book," it's so much more! It can become a *powerful* force in our lives. **Romans 1:16** says the Gospel is the *power* of God for our salvation. The word here for "power" is the same Greek word that the English word "dynamite" comes from! God's Word is powerful to blow up unhealthy habits or life-ruts so we can move into God's fulfilling purposes for our life.

Hebrews 4:12 describes God's Word as *"living and active"*—it's more than ink on a page. On the contrary, its ideas can generate spiritual growth and life.

Psalm 119:105 tells us that God's Word directs our paths. It's like a map that helps us navigate life's rugged terrain.

In **Luke 4:1-12**, Jesus uses God's Word as a powerful weapon in fighting a spiritual battle against Satan. After fasting and praying for 40 days in the desert, Jesus felt vulnerable and physically weak. Seizing the opportunity to take advantage of the situation, Satan attacked Jesus with three temptations, all rooted in deception. And with every temptation, Jesus confronted Satan's lies with the truth of Scripture, saying *"It is written . . ."*

Jesus relied on the Word of God as His powerful and effective way out! In the same way, with every temptation, God promises to give us a *"way of escape"* (1 Corinthians 10:13). Jesus always employed this approach—with 100 percent success. Ponder that.

And you can do the same. Satan will tempt you and try to deceive you. He will try to destroy your relationship with God and others. But God has given you His Word to combat the enemy's attacks.

Romans 12:2 addresses our need to have our minds renewed. Reading and meditating on Scripture is one of the best ways to renew our minds. As we allow scriptural truths to permeate our thinking, the lies Satan tells us are destroyed.

If you are consistently reading your Bible, your mind will be filled with God's higher ways and thoughts (Isaiah 55:8-9). If you are not, you are highly susceptible to the lies of the enemy. Your first line of defense and your spiritual nourishment rely upon getting God's Word into your heart and mind.

Consistently filling your mind with God's Word "reprograms" the many false beliefs that we have unknowingly accepted over time. **Ephesians 5:26** refers to it as *"the washing with water through the Word."* Get this—God's Word purifies and detoxifies your mind. You have heard of a "blood transfusion." Saturating yourself in Scripture gives you a "mind transfusion." By continually applying the Word of God to your life, you will be able to *"have the same mindset as Christ Jesus"* (Philippians 2:5).

bible reading and study tips

Here are some quick tips to help you get more out of the time you invest in studying God's Word:

1. Start in the Gospels. If you are a fairly new Christian, start with the book of Mark in the New Testament and read about Christ's life and ministry. Then try Acts, a book about the lives of the first Christians. Maybe head next to James, Philippians, or Ephesians for some practical tips on Christian living. Then see where God leads you next.

2. Set a time. Make a decision about when you will read your Bible, and then be faithful to that time. Treat it like an agreement to meet a friend. That is really what it is. Many meet with God and read his Word first thing in the morning because their minds are fresher and undistracted.

If you have trouble focusing in the morning, make time for God at the end of your day—or perhaps somewhere in the middle. But you should know that there is something about meeting with God at the start of each day, before doing anything else, that helps guide and position us to walk with Him all day long.

3. Write it down. Expect to hear from God when you read His Word. And when you do, write down what He says to you. You will forget much of what you *don't* write down. But you can repeatedly review what you *do* write down.

Make it a new habit to always have your *Spiritual Life Notebook* open and a pen handy when you are studying Scripture. We have provided pages in this section for you to write down what you are learning.

4. Start with prayer. Before you dive into the Word, ask God to make it come alive to you. Ask Him to teach you through it. Ask Him to show you how the passage you are reading applies to your life.

His Spirit is with you as you engage with His Word, and He wants to give you insights that you will never come up with on your own. He wants to open your mind so you can understand the Scriptures—just as Jesus did with the disciples in Luke 24:45.

5. Write *in* your Bible. The Bible is not a religious relic—it is a book that you read and reread throughout your life. And although it contains the words of life, it is still just leather and paper. Or as Forge speaker Adrian Despres says, "It's a tree between two cows."

You will get more out of your reading if you engage and interact with it. Here are a few suggestions in getting started:

Place **stars** next to verses that speak to you. One star might represent a verse worth recalling while 4 stars might be a life-long verse to remember. You can set the level of stars according to their importance to you.

? Draw a **question mark** where you don't understand something. Seek answers to your question with a pastor, commentary, or mature Christian friend.

Ⓜ Put an "M" next to a verse you want to memorize. Write out the chapter and verse of other passages that have similar messages.

◯ Underline or circle words that jump out at you. It can be especially helpful to also write the date next to particularly meaningful passages to help you remember when God spoke to you through it.

✎ Write thoughts and comments in the margins. Then use your *Spiritual Life Notebook* to write out more complete notes.

6. Get a modern translation. The King James Version of the Bible sounds poetic, but it is not always easy to understand. You may want to get a more modern translation that is written in today's language. Try a *Student Bible, Christian Standard Bible,* or the *New Living Translation*. Each is a reputable contemporary translation.

7. Memorize Scripture. Life is a spiritual battleground, and God's Word is one of our greatest offensive weapons. Going into life without God's Word stored in our minds and hearts is like going into battle with our hands tied behind our backs. Satan wants to keep us spiritually weak. But knowing Scripture by memory is a powerful way to fight his lies and attacks. That is why we have included a Scripture memorization record in this section.

8. Keep learning. There are countless methods and study aids online and at Christian bookstores for reading and studying the Bible. Discover with God ways that resonate with you and fit. Some people read a chapter from more than one book each day. Others read a lot one day, then meditate on one particular verse the next. Some study a whole book at once, others study a theme throughout the Bible (like "love" or "grace") and use a concordance to find the theme's verse locations.

Each method has different strengths and advantages in getting the most out of your study. Regardless of your method, what is most important is that you are filling your heart and mind with God's Word.

my bible study notes

This section contains pages for you to write down the things you are learning as you study God's Word. Here are some brief instructions to help you use these pages:

1. Fill in the date. This helps you track what God has taught you from week to week, month to month, year to year.

2. Fill in the passage. This is the Scripture you read for this study entry. Documenting this will allow you to more easily locate it later on when you want to find that particular study and the insights you gleaned from it.

3. Answer the study questions. If you do not have another Bible-study format, a simple one is provided for you on each Bible-study page. It includes categorical questions (Head, Heart, Hands, Feet) that will help you better understand, remember, and apply it to your life.

4. Note any questions you have and any Scriptures that stand out to memorize. Notating questions you have as you study will help you keep track, so, when you have opportunity, you can discuss with your spiritual mentor, pastor, or brother or sister in Christ.

My Bible Study

Scripture Passage: _____ Date: _____

1. **HEAD: What is this passage saying?** What is the main message? What do I learn about God—the Father, Jesus, the Holy Spirit—or people, creation, evil, etc.?

2. **HEART: What is God speaking to me, or how did this impact me personally?** What part sticks out to me? What changes do I need to make in my beliefs, attitudes, actions?

3. **HANDS: This very week, how will I practically obey what God has shown me?** What next step will I take?

4. **FEET: Who will I share with?** Is there anyone in my life that I need to tell about what I learned to encourage them?

_____

_____

_____

_____

_____

_____

_____

_____

_____

_____

_____

_____

Question(s) to ask my spiritual mentor regarding this:

_____

_____

_____

_____

_____

Verses to memorize:

_____

_____

reading through the bible tips

The Bible tells a whole story. That is why it's important to read the whole story. For the same reason we would not read half a novel or watch bits and pieces of a movie or just pay attention to selective portions of our life—reading *all* of God's Word is important in knowing the fullness of all He wants to do in and through us.

While we do not get "extra credit" for reading God's Word cover to cover, we do get a more accurate understanding of who God is, how He has worked in history, what His plans are for the present and future, and how we fit into those plans.

Some portions of God's Word are easier to read and seem more relevant to our personal situation. Other portions seem obscure and harder to understand. Still, all of God's Word matters and the more we engage His Word, the more we know Him and mature in Him.

Here is one way to keep track of where you have been and where you would like to go in reading God's Word. Simply cross off or highlight each chapter as you read. It takes the guesswork out of wondering, "Have I read that book or chapter?"

B.Y.O.B. and Hybrid Approaches:

Many apps and forms exist to help you know what you have read in the Bible. Plans for reading the Bible in a year (or three years) are also plentiful. Maybe you are already using a plan for reading and recording what you have read. Great! Don't stop! These forms are here to serve you. Adapt them to meet *your* needs in a way that will keep you motivated and growing.

Remember: Getting *up-close* with God, not getting *uptight* about forms, is always the goal!

Old Testament

	1	2	3	4	5	6	7	8	9	10	11	12	13	14	15	16	17	18
Genesis	19	20	21	22	23	24	25	26	27	28	29	30	31	32	33	34	35	36
	39	40	41	42	43	44	45	46	47	48	49	50						
Exodus	1	2	3	4	5	6	7	8	9	10	11	12	13	14	15	16	17	18
	19	20	21	22	23	24	25	26	27	28	29	30	31	32	33	34	35	36
	39	40																
Leviticus	1	2	3	4	5	6	7	8	9	10	11	12	13	14	15	16	17	18
	19	20	21	22	23	24	25	26	27									
Numbers	1	2	3	4	5	6	7	8	9	10	11	12	13	14	15	16	17	18
	19	20	21	22	23	24	25	26	27	28	29	30	31	32	33	34	35	36
Deuteronomy	1	2	3	4	5	6	7	8	9	10	11	12	13	14	15	16	17	18
	19	20	21	22	23	24	25	26	27	28	29	30	31	32	33	34		
Joshua	1	2	3	4	5	6	7	8	9	10	11	12	13	14	15	16	17	18
	19	20	21	22	23	24												
Judges	1	2	3	4	5	6	7	8	9	10	11	12	13	14	15	16	17	18
	19	20	21															
Ruth	1	2	3	4														
1 Samuel	1	2	3	4	5	6	7	8	9	10	11	12	13	14	15	16	17	18
	19	20	21	22	23	24	25	26	27	28	29	30	31					
2 Samuel	1	2	3	4	5	6	7	8	9	10	11	12	13	14	15	16	17	18
	19	20	21	22	23	24												
1 Kings	1	2	3	4	5	6	7	8	9	10	11	12	13	14	15	16	17	18
	19	20	21	22														
2 Kings	1	2	3	4	5	6	7	8	9	10	11	12	13	14	15	16	17	18
	19	20	21	22	23	24	25											
1 Chronicles	1	2	3	4	5	6	7	8	9	10	11	12	13	14	15	16	17	18
	19	20	21	22	23	24	25	26	27	28	29							
2 Chronicles	1	2	3	4	5	6	7	8	9	10	11	12	13	14	15	16	17	18
	19	20	21	22	23	24	25	26	27	28	29	30	31	32	33	34	35	36
Ezra	1	2	3	4	5	6	7	8	9	10								
Nehemiah	1	2	3	4	5	6	7	8	9	10	11	12	13					
Esther	1	2	3	4	5	6	7	8	9	10								
Job	1	2	3	4	5	6	7	8	9	10	11	12	13	14	15	16	17	18
	19	20	21	22	23	24	25	26	27	28	29	30	31	32	33	34	35	36
	37	38	39	40	41	42												

Old Testament

Psalms																	
1	2	3	4	5	6	7	8	9	10	11	12	13	14	15	16	17	18
19	20	21	22	23	24	25	26	27	28	29	30	31	32	33	34	35	36
37	38	39	40	41	42	43	44	45	46	47	48	49	50	51	52	53	54
55	56	57	58	59	60	61	62	63	64	65	66	67	68	69	70	71	72
73	74	75	76	77	78	79	80	81	82	83	84	85	86	87	88	89	90
91	92	93	94	95	96	97	98	99	100	101	102	103	104	105	106	107	108
109	110	111	112	113	114	115	116	117	118	119	120	121	122	123	124	125	126
127	128	129	130	131	132	133	134	135	136	137	138	139	140	141	142	143	144
145	146	147	148	149	150												

Proverbs: 1 2 3 4 5 6 7 8 9 10 11 12 13 14 15 16 17 18 19 20 21 22 23 24 25 26 27 28 29 30 31

Ecclesiastes: 1 2 3 4 5 6 7 8 9 10 11 12

Song of Songs: 1 2 3 4 5 6 7 8

Isaiah: 1 2 3 4 5 6 7 8 9 10 11 12 13 14 15 16 17 18 19 20 21 22 23 24 25 26 27 28 29 30 31 32 33 34 35 36 37 38 39 40 41 42 43 44 45 46 47 48 49 50 51 52 53 54 55 56 57 58 59 60 61 62 63 64 65 66

Jeremiah: 1 2 3 4 5 6 7 8 9 10 11 12 13 14 15 16 17 18 19 20 21 22 23 24 25 26 27 28 29 30 31 32 33 34 35 36 37 38 39 40 41 42 43 44 45 46 47 48 49 50 51 52

Lamentations: 1 2 3 4 5

Ezekiel: 1 2 3 4 5 6 7 8 9 10 11 12 13 14 15 16 17 18 19 20 21 22 23 24 25 26 27 28 29 30 31 32 33 34 35 36 37 38 39 40 41 42 43 44 45 46 47 48

Daniel: 1 2 3 4 5 6 7 8 9 10 11 12

Hosea: 1 2 3 4 5 6 7 8 9 10 11 12 13 14

Joel: 1 2 3

Amos: 1 2 3 4 5 6 7 8 9

Obadiah: 1

Jonah: 1 2 3 4

Micah: 1 2 3 4

Nahum: 1 2 3

Habakkuk: 1 2 3

Zephaniah: 1 2 3

Haggai: 1 2

Zechariah: 1 2 3 4 5 6 7 8 9 10 11 12 13 14

Malachi: 1 2 3 4

New Testament

Matthew	1	2	3	4	5	6	7	8	9	10	11	12	13	14	15	16
	17	18	19	20	21	22	23	24	25	26	27	28	29	30		
Mark	1	2	3	4	5	6	7	8	9	10	11	12	13	14	15	16
Luke	1	2	3	4	5	6	7	8	9	10	11	12	13	14	15	16
	17	18	19	20	21	22	23	24								
John	1	2	3	4	5	6	7	8	9	10	11	12	13	14	15	16
	17	18	19	20	21											
Acts	1	2	3	4	5	6	7	8	9	10	11	12	13	14	15	16
		19	20	21	22	23	24	25	26	27	28					
Romans	1	2	3	4	5	6	7	8	9	10	11	12	13	14	15	16
1 Corinthians	1	2	3	4	5	6	7	8	9	10	11	12	13	14	15	16
2 Corinthians	1	2	3	4	5	6	7	8	9	10	11	12	13			
Galatians	1	2	3	4	5	6										
Ephesians	1	2	3	4	5	6										
Philippians	1	2	3	4												
Colossians	1	2	3	4												
1 Thessalonians	1	2	3	4												
2 Thessalonians	1	2	3													
1 Timothy	1	2	3	4	5	6										
2 Timothy	1	2	3	4												
Titus	1	2	3													
Philemon	1															
Hebrews	1	2	3	4	5	6	7	8	9	10	11					
James	1	2	3	4	5											
1 Peter	1	2	3	4	5											
2 Peter	1	2	3													
1 John	1	2	3	4	5											
2 John	1															
3 John	1															
Jude	1															
Revelation	1	2	3	4	5	6	7	8	9	10	11	12	13	14	15	16
	17	18	19	20	21	22										

my scripture memorization

Memorizing God's Word is one of the most powerfully life-changing things we can ever do! Here, you will find a form to help track your Scripture memorization and make organizing and reviewing your Scripture memory work easy. At the back of this book, you will find Scripture memory verses prepared for you with a selection of the most important and treasured passages followers of Jesus have been memorizing and standing upon for centuries.

Here are some brief instructions to help you with memorizing Scripture:

1. Decide what to memorize. Record the verses you want to memorize as they come to you through Bible study, prayer, a sermon, or even a challenge from a mentor or friend. As you determine meaningful, helpful, and needed verses, write down the *Scripture Reference* and the *Date Started* on your form. You may find it helpful to start with the selection of memory verse cards provided for you at the back of this book.

2. Begin memorizing. Go at a pace that works for you. This isn't a race or competition. It is a chance to absorb God's Word into you, so you are transformed and ready—to face life's challenges, to serve God faithfully, offer hope and life to others, and to enjoy God!

Here are a few tips:

- You *can* memorize Scripture, and your life will be enriched for doing so. When memorizing a new passage, one of the most helpful starting points is to read the passage 10 times in a row, write the passage 10 times in a row, and finally, speak the passage 10 times in a row. This will get it into your short-term memory.

- Another technique is to emphasize a different word each time you say the verse, doing this with every word. It's amazing how this will rearrange the meaning of the verse to you, and make it so much easier to learn the whole verse! For example Matthew 7:7:

"ASK and it will be given to you . . ."
"Ask and IT will be given to you . . ."
"Ask and it WILL be given to you . . ."
"Ask and it will BE GIVEN to you . . ."
"Ask and it will be given to YOU . . ."

- Once a passage is in your short-term memory, you can continue to memorize it while standing in a line, sitting in a waiting room, waiting in traffic, cleaning, jogging, etc. Try writing out a verse and putting it in your wallet or purse. Place it in your phone, tablet, or smart watch and set a reminder. Maybe write the verse on your bathroom mirror or car window with a dry erase marker. Get creative! Review the verse(s) whenever you get a few free moments. Over time, this will get them into your long-term memory.

- The Holy Spirit will help you do this! You will find that as you work to memorize a passage, God will bring it to life in your everyday experience. You will see Scripture come alive before your eyes and understand it like never before!

3. Record and celebrate what you have memorized. Record the date you completed memorizing the passage. Give God thanks and celebrate with each verse memorized that more of God and His Word are inside you!

4. Note uses for the verses. As you add new verses to memorize, take time to recall the verses you have already memorized. Noting uses or topics for verses will help you do this. Try to capture the purpose of the verse in a word or two, for example, "Peace." Periodically, see if you remember the verses as well as you once did. If so, great! If not, no worries—use the time to refresh your memory and reflect on the passages.

My Scripture Memory			
Scripture	Date Started	Date Memorized	Uses for This Verse

sermon listening tips

God often speaks to us through spiritually gifted teachers and pastors who inspire, challenge, encourage, correct, and edify us through the proclamation of His Word.

Gifted preachers and teachers can make the Bible come alive in fresh and new ways, helping us see how God's ancient truth powerfully applies to our lives. Through them, God often speaks life-changing truths.

One definition of a sermon is "Sharing God's truth in contemporary ways." That means the task of the preacher (message-giver or speaker) is to spend time with God and His Word, do the work of carefully understanding what God is saying through the sermon text, and share the message carefully, prayerfully, and faithfully in ways the sermon hearers can comprehend, relate to, and respond.

The job of the sermon deliverer is serious business and requires a lot of investment! That makes sermon listening an important task too. Regardless of your interest in the topic, God likely has something in mind for you.

Listen with *expectancy* to the sermon or teaching and believe you will receive what you need to grow *deeper* in your relationship with God. You'll be amazed at how much better speakers will speak once you begin taking notes! You will discover that something can be gained from even the dullest and driest speakers as you take notes. Content is often rich despite dry delivery.

As you listen with Bible, pen, and notebook in hand, God will see your expectant posture of readiness. And He is a giver! He delights in helping and blessing people who are prepared to receive from Him! Here are some tips to help you get the most out of sermon listening:

1. **Pray for the messenger and message**. Before you listen, pray that God *will speak* to the messenger. Then pray that you *will hear* what God speaks through that messenger.

2. Write down the message. Don't assume that you will remember what you *hear* in a sermon. Studies indicate that we forget more than 90 percent of a sermon within two days after it is given. You may remember the big idea and perhaps one or two of the stories, but that is about it.

Record the name of the person, message title, and date. This information is helpful in case you decide to secure an audio recording of the message for you or someone else at a later date. Keep in mind that the more thorough your notes are, the more you will benefit when you review them—and they will be much more helpful when you share them with someone else.

Develop your own personal marking system while taking notes (i.e. a star for important personal insights, a circle around practical ideas, a box around a profound quote)— to quickly locate them later for review, filing, or sharing with someone else.

Realize that once you write it down, you can return to it again and again—for your own good and for others.

3. Apply the message. Many people seek out churches with uniquely gifted preachers and teachers in the pulpit, and subscribe to podcasts of their favorite national speakers—allowing them to hear the latest and greatest thinking on various aspects of the Christian faith.

But unfortunately, those profound insights may never move beyond our ears, penetrating our hearts and affecting our everyday lives.

God never intended for us to merely hear the Word—He wants us to live it, to do it! James 1:22-25 promises a *doer* (not simply a *hearer*) "will be blessed in what he does."

As the sermon wraps up—before the closing prayer, before you leave the building—write a one-sentence summary at the end of your notes and an idea or two on how you can implement what you have learned in the message.

Then, over the next week, do your best to apply what you have learned to your life.

my sermon notes

The sermon notes form in this section is designed so you can use it in church—or wherever else you might hear God's Word proclaimed—and write down what God is speaking to you.

Here are some brief instructions to help with this form:

1. Fill in the Date. This helps you track what God has taught you from week to week, month to month, year to year.

2. Fill in the Speaker, Text, and Topic. The *Speaker* is the name of the person giving the message. The *Text* is the book, chapter, and verses of the sermon. The *Topic* is a word or phrase on what the sermon is about (like "Forgiveness").

3. Notes. As you listen to the sermon, write down what you believe the speaker is communicating, things you hear God saying to you, and anything else you think is important.

4. Summary and Life Application. Write a one-sentence summary after the sermon. This will keep the message in your mind longer. Then, write your life application. What are some practical ways you can apply the message to your life and put them in action in the week (or months) ahead?

My Sermon Notes

Speaker: _____   Text: _____

Date: _____   Topic: _____

_____
_____
_____
_____
_____
_____
_____
_____
_____
_____
_____
_____
_____
_____
_____
_____

Summary *(In one sentence, the main thing God is saying to me through this sermon is . . .)*

_____
_____
_____
_____

Life Application *(The action steps I want to take are . . .)*

_____
_____
_____
_____

extra bible study approach: character study

You can use this extra section if you want to study a character in multiple places where they show up in Scripture.

Here are some brief instructions to help with this form:

1. Fill in the Bible character. This is the person you want to do the study on, such as Peter, John, Abraham, etc.

2. Fill in the date. This helps you track what God has taught you about this person over time. You don't have to complete your study all in one day! In fact, you may even find it helpful to complete this study over a period of time, coming to it with fresh eyes on various days.

3. Note the Scriptures. These are the Scriptures you are reading and drawing insights from for your study.

4. Record your insights. Ask the Holy Spirit to speak to you through this Biblical character's life. What can you learn from this mention of them as part of the larger Biblical story?

4. Summary and impact. Write a short summary of what you learned. What are some practical ways you can apply these principles to your life and put them in action in the week (or months) ahead?

Extra Bible Study Approach: Character Study		
Bible Character:		
Date:	Scripture:	Insight:
Summary of insights, key takeaways, and impact on my life:		

extra bible study approach: topic/word study

You can use this extra section if you want to study a particular topic or word throughout Scripture.

Here are some brief instructions to help with this form:

1. Fill in the Bible topic or word. This is what you want to do the study on, such as forgiveness, hope, light, etc.

2. Fill in the date. This helps you track what God has taught you about this topic or word over time. You don't have to complete your study all in one day! In fact, you may even find it helpful to complete this study over a period of time, coming to it with fresh eyes on various days.

3. Note the Scriptures. These are the Scriptures you are reading and drawing insights from for your study.

4. Record your insights. Ask the Holy Spirit to speak to you. What can you learn from this topic or word when you study it as part of the larger Biblical story?

4. Summary and impact. Write a short summary of what you learned. What are some practical ways you can apply these principles to your life and put them in action in the week (or months) ahead?

Extra Bible Study Approach: Topic/Word Study		
Topic/Word:		
Date:	Scripture:	Insight:
Summary of insights, key takeaways, and impact on my life:		

further resources on god's word

Capture the QR Code below to access the Spiritual Life Notebook resource page or go to: www.ForgeForward.org/SLN.

You will find:

- Printable My Bible Study, My Scripture Memory, My Sermon Notes, Character Study, and Topic/Word Study journal pages.
- A how-to video on Bible study, Bible reading, and Scripture memory.
- Link to the Navigator's Topical Memory System, one of the best-loved Scripture memory courses of all time!
- Free audiobook of the resource *Forged by Fire.* What if God really is trustworthy? What if, up close to the fire of His love, He warms your heart and shapes your life for the wonder and purpose always meant for you? What if your intimacy with Him actually becomes your greatest gift to the world? Isn't that a fire worth running to and a forge worth entering? Best of all – get this: God warmly invites you, "Come!"

up-close in prayer

. . .

engaging prayer as a lifestyle

Consider the closest relationships you have. They didn't get that way through occasional, "because we have to" exchanges. You're most likely well-connected because of frequent exchanges over a long period of time. Quality time and conversation with people you love makes deeper, meaningful relationships.

In a nutshell, that's prayer: a lifestyle of constant connection and deeper conversation with God.

Prayer isn't an add-on. It's not something one does when things go especially bad or seem to be extraordinarily good. Prayer is a constant communication exchange with God. Prayer is both praying at meal times and praying on your commute to work or school. It's conversation with God wherever you find yourself, whenever you sense God's presence, see a need, or simply want to express your affection toward Him. Prayer is not something so much we "do," but something we live —ongoing connection, communication, speaking and listening with God.

Superheroes

People love superheroes. We always have. Superheroes even date back to the days before Greek mythology. They appear in the folklore of nearly every culture as well as many popular TV shows and movies.

Mythical stories about superheroes are everywhere.

Iron Man, Wonder Woman, Black Panther, Spiderman, Hulk—sound familiar? They're just a handful of many. Maybe you carried them to school on your lunchbox or remembered them at night as they adorned your pajamas or hovered over you in poster form on the wall.

And Superman. Remember him? He was one of the most popular superheroes of the 20th century.

Ever wonder why Superman was so appealing? Perhaps because Clark Kent was just an ordinary guy like the rest of us. But when trouble appeared, he would step into a telephone booth, and voila, Superman showed up.

No one can explain what happened to Clark in that phone booth, but we do know that he was somehow transformed into a powerful force against evil.

Becoming A Superhero

Despite the abundance of superheroes in television, comic books, and costume stores, the world actually needs more. Not the mythical kind, though. It needs real superheroes—ordinary Christians who transform into supermen, superwomen, and superkids as they enter—not a phone booth—but their "prayer closets" of constant connection with God. Superheroes who defeat dark forces on their knees.

Prayer *really does* transform ordinary men, women, and children into superheroes! Prayer partners us with God to do what is humanly impossible. And, it makes our enemy, Satan, tremble and retreat.

That's why Satan tries so hard to keep Christians from entering their "prayer closets." He knows that a prayerless Christian is a powerless Christian. But a praying Christian has superhero capacity to bring God's plans, purposes, and power to earth.

No wonder Satan trembles when we pray!

prayer tips

Here are some quick tips that will help your prayer life become more powerful and effective:

1. Keep it real.

Satan wants to convince you that prayer is more complicated than it really is. But it's not all that complex—it's just honest, two-way communication between you and your heavenly Father.

Sometimes it involves confessing sin, other times it means asking God for your needs or the needs of others, or thanking him for all you have, or telling him how you feel. And sometimes it means listening to God's guidance in your life.

But at its heart, prayer is honest communication with God.

God doesn't require perfect sentence structure and religious-sounding words. He wants to hear what's *really* on your heart. It's okay if you sit in silence and think. It makes no difference to Him if you stumble trying to find the right words to express what's going on inside. Your profound words won't impress Him, anyway. What matters most is engaging God with your head, your heart, and your spirit.

God is drawn to honest humility (1 Peter 5:5). So keep it humble and keep it real.

2. Write it down.

Keep a record of your prayers in a prayer list or journal because God answers them according to His timetable—not ours—which means it may take a while. Writing them down will help you remember what you prayed and how God answered.

Over time, you will become more and more amazed at how many prayers God answered. And as you re-read your record of God's many answered prayers, you will find the encouragement to pray with more faith in the future.

That's why a prayer list is included in this section. You can write down your prayer requests and record God's answers. Over time, you will build a growing reminder of God's faithfulness . . . simply by keeping a record.

3. Pray without ceasing.

The Bible says to "pray without ceasing" (1 Thessalonians 5:17). This means acknowledging God's presence all the time—and not ignoring Him. Imagine how you'd feel if whenever you spent time with your friends, they acted as if you weren't there?

God surrounds you with His presence throughout your day and He promises to never leave you (see Deuteronomy 31:8). So share your day with Him.

You can "pray without ceasing" by simply speaking to God as you think of things. You don't have to wait for a "quiet time" to share your thoughts.

If you are enjoying your day, tell Him. If you are stressed out or afraid, cast your cares on Him. If you are thinking about others, pray for them. If you are talking with someone else, ask God to speak through you. If you are thankful for something, direct your thankfulness to God. If He speaks to you, give Him your attention. That is what it means to pray without ceasing.

4. Listen without ceasing.

Don't only *speak* as you pray without ceasing, but *listen* without ceasing too. Listen for God's voice throughout your day, and then write down what He says to you. He may speak to you about yourself, another person, or something He wants you to do.

Take the time to listen. And then follow through on what He shares with you. Remember, prayer is two-way communication with God. Keep listening for His voice.

5. Be specific.

All of us have prayed the "Bless . . ." and "Be with . . ." prayers. They're easy! And they're a great way to economize on time and energy.

But when we offer ambiguous prayers like "Bless Grandpa Joe . . ." or "Be with my friend Chris . . ." we never see the *specific* details of how God answered our prayers in the lives of our friends. In the end, they do little to build our faith.

Yet, when we ask God to show us how to pray *specific* prayers for *specific* people in *specific* situations, we clearly see how God *specifically* answers our prayers. Our faith grows as a result of seeing them answered. And God gets the glory for answering our prayers!

6. Keep your promises.

Never tell someone you will pray for them (or their prayer request) if you don't intend to really pray. In the effort of being polite, you may actually break a promise. They are counting on you to pray!

When someone asks you to pray for something, write it down *immediately*—in their presence. If you don't, you will likely forget. When you write it down in front of them, you communicate that their request is important to you.

And don't share their prayer requests with others if it is not the loving thing to do. Otherwise, you may be guilty of gossiping—which may actually hurt the people you claim to be helping through your prayers.

7. Be a lifetime student of prayer.

Prayer played a central role in Jesus' life and ministry on earth. It also played a central role in the lives of His disciples. They did not ask Jesus to teach them how to teach, preach, or sing. They asked Him to teach them how to pray (Luke 11:1). They knew its importance in their life and ministry and witnessed firsthand its impact when Jesus turned His attention heavenward in prayer.

We, too, need to be lifetime students of prayer. Practicing prayer, studying Scripture, and reading books on prayer are great ways to do this. Some of my favorite books include *Touch the World Through Prayer* and *Mighty Prevailing Prayer* by Wesley Duewel; *Fresh Wind, Fresh Fire* by Jim Cymbala; and *Victorious Praying* by Bill Thrasher.

You can also download my audio resource on prayer and praise entitled "Two Wings that Soar" on the Forge App. Search for "Forging Lives" in the App Store and look for the section "In App Content to Forge Your Life."

You can also get the app via this link: TheForgeApp.com.

a helpful guide to praying

Prayer is conversation with God. It's communication at the heart level —speaking, listening, exchanging thoughts, ideas, instructions.

Communicating with God is much like communicating with others— the more you practice it, the better you become at it. That said, prayer can be awkward, especially at first. It's also easy to make our prayers all about us.

Here is one way we have found helpful to create healthy and balanced habits in prayer. It keeps our focus on God and His plans, purposes, and activity in our lives and in His Kingdom. While this is only one path to prayer, so many excellent ways to connect with God through prayer have been discovered and taught throughout the centuries. Let the Holy Spirit lead you!

P.R.A.Y.

P – Praise. Think about what it means to "adore" or "praise" someone you love and respect. How much more should we do that with God! Let your praise and adoration flow to our very great, good, gracious, and glorious God!

If I believe God to be the one who heals, I tell Him, "God, You are healer. You are the One who restores. You are the One that does it all. You are sovereign in my life."

Praise deposits the truth of who God is into your heart and reminds you of who God is supposed to be in your life. Praise is about letting God know, and really about reminding ourselves, of who He is, of how big He is, and of what He has done in our lives.

When we learn to praise God and lift Him up, He lifts our perspective up out of the muck of the situation that we are in, whatever we might be facing, whatever we might be struggling with. As you praise God, lifting Him up in your own heart and in your own life, He lifts you to see glimpses of your life and circumstance from His vantage point.

When we praise God, our joy is more full, and our enjoyment of Him is greater! Thank God—for everything, everyone, every situation and circumstance.

R – Repent. God wants us to come before Him with a clear conscience and with open eyes . . . *"Lord, forgive our trespasses as we forgive those who have trespassed against us. And lead us not into temptation but deliver us from evil"* (Matthew 6:12-14).

As we take a humble posture coming before God, and we remember who He is, all of a sudden, He shines His light into our life. We need to be honest with ourselves as God convicts us, and we realize, *I need to turn it around here. I need to change this. I need to give this to God.* When God shines His light into our life, He exposes the dead things, wounds, and pain, and He begins to clean them out so we can be refreshed and renewed.

Confess to God where you have missed it with Him and others when it comes to personal shortcomings, or the hurt and pain you may be carrying from someone else. And ask Him to forgive you. Forgive those who have wronged you. Ask God to turn your life and gaze in the right direction, so that as you live in the mainstreams of life, you can live with clean hands and a pure heart.

A – Ask. Scripture declares, *"You do not have because you do not ask"* (James 4:2-3). We may ask for things that we need or desire to see happen! God wants us to ask Him and as we do, there is an abundance of provision in Him. While God invites us to ask Him to *"give us this day our daily bread,"* (Matthew 6:11) this does not mean He is going to give us everything we want. We yield to His will, no matter what that is.

Pray for the needs, healing, and wholeness, of yourself and others. Pray for the salvation of the world, your country, your city, your neighborhood. Pray for God's Kingdom and His Church. Pray for anyone, any situation, anything God puts on your heart. Ask Him to restore and have His way. And, ask how you can join Him in what He is up to in these things.

Y – Yield. Jesus modeled the prayer *"Not My will but Yours be done"* (Luke 22:42). As we go through the process of praising, of repenting, of asking, we leave the rest in God's hands We may not understand what is going on in a situation we are facing, but at some point, we just have to say, *God, you know best. And after I have talked to You, and after I have done all the work of searching the Scriptures, I yield to You. Not my will, but Your will be done.*

There are things you are going to ask God for, and He is going to say "No," or He may say, "Not right now." And when we attempt to force God to do things outside of His timing, we get ourselves in trouble. God always has a plan, yet we may not understand. God always has an intention that we may not know. And His ways are higher than our ways. So, at some point, we look at what God is doing and say, "Okay, God, I yield to You."

In yielding, we also listen for His voice, leading, and prompting. He may speak through: a Scripture verse, a still small whisper or prompting thought, a heavy-hearted burden that leads you to action, or even an image such as a vision or dream. When you hear something that might be from God, write it down. Whatever our yielding through listening looks like, it must always line up with the Word of God!

And so, this is how we can follow a simple pattern, praying as Jesus taught us: Praise. Repent. Ask. Yield . . . P.R.A.Y.

my prayer journal

Discover an opportunity to record your prayers in journal form. Some people feel they express themselves more easily when writing out their prayers. Others prefer the prayer list format. You can use one or both types of prayer pages. Here are a couple of tips for journaling your prayers:

1. Date your entries. This enables you to review the work God has done in your life through your prayers.

2. P.R.A.Y. In your entry, consider going through the PRAY acronym to help you pray holistically and in line with God's heart as you connect with Him.

3. Express your honest feelings and include specific details. The prayer journal is ideal for writing out the personal feelings behind your prayers. It can serve as a therapeutic release of stress, doubt, or pain. As you write them down, release those emotions to God, and ask Him to replace your burdens with joy and peace. Journaling your prayers naturally makes room for you to go into greater detail regarding your request—which in turn brings greater joy when God answers your prayer. Over time, it becomes a living archive of your walk with God.

5. Listen and write what God may be saying. Spend time listening. Write down what God brings to mind. He may speak through: a Scripture verse, a still small whisper or prompting thought, a heavy-hearted burden that leads you to action, or even an image such as a vision or dream. Write it down, pray over it in response, and entrust the result to God!

6. Keep it safe. If you do use a prayer journal to more fully express your feelings and prayer life, you will want to keep it in a safe place. You may want to keep this section in your home—so you don't leave it somewhere. This will help you guard your privacy and the privacy of those you are praying for. God may on occasion share a prayer concern with you that is for you and Him alone.

My Prayer Journal

Date: _____

"Lord, what I want to share with You r ght now is..."

Date: _____

"Lord, what I want to share with You right now is..."

my prayer list

This "Prayer List" template provides a way for you to keep a written record of your prayer requests. Here are some instructions for using it:

1. Enter the date. The date is important because it helps you see how quickly God answers some of your prayers, and it helps you to persevere in prayer over time. When God answers, it fuels your faith for the next time.

2. Fill out your request. Albert Einstein once said, "Everything should be made as simple as possible, but not simpler." As you fill out your prayer request, it can be short, but include enough of the details so you can remember when you look back a few weeks or months later.

3. Remember to record your answers to prayer. This will build your faith and increase your desire to pray diligently! Review this column frequently to remember all God has done.

4. Organize your pages. You can organize your prayer pages in whatever way works best for you. Some people keep one list for their own needs and separate lists for friends, family, neighbors, etc. Some keep different pages of requests for different kinds of prayer requests.

As you fill up the answer column, keep answered original pages as a lifelong record of God's faithfulness.

B.Y.O.B. and Hybrid Approaches:

As always, use these journal pages to best serve *your* needs. If you already have a prayer notebook or a way of storing your prayer needs electronically—fantastic! Simply adapt the My Prayer List concepts to what you are already doing. Remember: getting *up-close* with God is always the goal, not getting *uptight* about forms!

My Prayer List

Request Date: _____   Answer Date: _____

Request:

Answer:

Request Date: _____   Answer Date: _____

Request:

Answer:

Request Date: _____   Answer Date: _____

Request:

Answer:

further resources on prayer

Capture the QR Code below to access the Spiritual Life Notebook resource page or go to: www.ForgeForward.org/SLN.

You will find:

- Printable My Prayer Journal and My Prayer List journal pages.
- A downloadable, free eBook of the resource *Is God Waiting for a Date with You?* Through personal stories, practical tips, and easy-to-follow instruction, discover what "Dates Alone with God" are and how you can engage, enjoy, and benefit from them.
- Link to the Forge App where you can find the teaching "Two Wings that Soar: The Power of Prayer and Praise."

up-close in reflection

. . .

engaging reflection as a lifestyle

Have you ever considered how a person improves at anything? A job, singing, sports, finances, education, getting healthy and fit . . . really just about anything you can imagine. We get better, grow, move forward, and get places when we take time to evaluate where we have been, where we are, and the adjustments needed to take us where we want to be.

The same is true in your relationship with Jesus.

When you said "yes" to Jesus' invitation to be in relationship with Him, that was not the finish line. On the contrary. Your race had just begun. Just as a person has a whole lifetime ahead after being physically born, so it is with Jesus when a person is spiritually born. A lifetime of learning, growing, enjoying, serving, pleasing, and yes, maturing in Jesus comes after commitment to Him as Savior and Lord. Saying "yes" to Jesus is saying "yes" to a daily life *with* Him for the remainder of your life and into eternity.

That's exciting news! A daily life with God is a "get to" not a "have to." It is knowing God more and more as you daily live, love, and serve *with* Him.

Part of that daily growth and maturing (like an infant to an adult, like a sapling to a full-grown tree, like a first date to a seasoned marriage) is daily pausing and assessing how things are going.

Regular reflection with Jesus is much more than something we do at weekend times of worship. It is a lifestyle of walking with and checking in with Jesus day-by-day, throughout the day. It is a "get to" for every serious follower of Jesus who wants to grow in his or her relationship with Him. It is the way we get to where we want to be!

reflection tips

Growth Markers with God

Most of us find it extremely easy to float through life without paying much attention to the ways we grow and change. Sometimes we make significant decisions to follow God's will, yet forget about them a few weeks or months later.

Think for a moment: When has God taught you a significant lesson that altered the way you live or changed the direction of your life?

Perhaps you are thinking of the time you gave your life to Jesus. Or when you decided to give up an addiction. Maybe you surrendered something to God that you had been holding on to. Or perhaps you decided to forgive.

These moments act as stepping-stones in our journey with God. We will never be perfect, but day-by-day, God calls us to dig deeper and go farther with Him. Recording our interactions with God, the decisions we make, and the lessons we learn can be extremely beneficial to our spiritual lives. It helps us remember the significant spiritual moments, motivates us to keep acting on them long after they occur, and provides a record of God's work that we can share with others to spiritually invest and mentor them in the faith!

Pursuing God

God pursues us, and He wants us to pursue Him as well. In fact, He has given us several promises that directly relate to our pursuit of Him.

He says, *"You will seek Me and find Me when you seek Me with all your heart"* (Jeremiah 29:13).

In this passage, God gives us two promises. First, He promises that we *will* find Him when we seek Him wholeheartedly. It doesn't say we *may* find Him. It says we *will*. That is a promise.

God gives us a similar promise later in Scripture: *"Come near to God and He will come near to you"* (James 4:8, emphasis added).

God *will* respond when we pursue Him.

But He also gives us a second promise in the Jeremiah 29 passage. God says that we will find *Him* when we seek Him. It doesn't say we will find out more *about Him*. It says we will find *Him*. We will find a personal God who wants to be known and wants to know us. And we will know Him better and deeper as we draw near to Him and seek after Him. That is a promise, too.

When you pursue Him, God *will* reveal Himself to you.

This section of *Up-Close: A Spiritual Life Notebook* is designed to help you actively, wholeheartedly, and continually pursue God—all the days of your life. It gives you a place to journal your thoughts and prayers as you communicate with Him, reflect on how you are living, and a record of your life-changing experiences as He calls you to deeper places in your relationship with Him.

Engaging God

Seeking God is not a one-time act. It is so much more than just seeking Him once, finding Him, and then forgetting about Him. We continually seek God over the course of a lifetime so that we may continue to discover the riches of knowing Him.

There will always be more of God to pursue and discover!

This section will also help you more fully engage with God over the course of time because it gives you a place to write down what He says to you and what you want to say to Him.

Engaging God requires that we focus our thoughts and express our feelings. It also requires check-ins and check-ups along the way. For many of us, we do this best when we write them down in a journal.

Remembering God

1 Chronicles 16:12 tells us, *"Remember the wonders He has done, His miracles, and the judgments He pronounced."*

In the Old Testament, God's people repeated the same mistake again and again—they forgot about God and what He had done for them. Their lack of reverence and remembrance offended Him and resulted in harmful consequences. The most devastating consequence, however, was the distance it created between them and God (see Isaiah 59:2).

We are no different. If we are God's people—which, if you are a follower of Jesus, you are—then we need to remember God and what He has done for us. And it is just as important to remember the "little" and seemingly insignificant things that He does for us every day. Both the big and small things point us to His character and remind us of His faithfulness.

This section is also designed to help you remember. It gives you a place to record what God is teaching you so you can review—and remember —it later.

As you re-read your entries, you will realize how your thoughts and feelings have changed over time. You will remember what He has brought you through, what He has provided for you and other loved ones, what He has taught you, and most of all, how much He loves you. It is like your very own spiritual autobiography!

When you fight discouragement, reading this section will make it impossible to deny what God has done in and through your life. And it will give you more courage to face your present circumstance as well as the challenges ahead. It will also provide stories of His faithfulness that you can share with others to help them grow in Christ too!

my weekly overview

Time is a precious commodity. Like a delicious apple pie, there is only so much time to divide and so many ways to divide it. The writer of Psalm 90 requests of the Lord, *"Teach us to number our days that we may gain a heart of wisdom"* (verse 12). My Weekly Overview is a way to help keep the main things the main things throughout your week.

1.   Fill in the date. This helps you track your growth from week to week, month to month, year to year.

2.   Verse of the Week. You may have a verse that jumped out at you during worship, Bible study, or randomly during the day. Or, you may want a reminder of who God is or something you are working on. If so, write it here.

3.   Daily Time with God. Prayerfully determine what time with God will look like for the week including what time of day you will meet with Him. The goal is to know Jesus and keep your meeting agreement with Him, not to check off all the boxes. Daily spending time up-close with Jesus will help you stay connected to Him and bear the fruit He desires through your life.

4.   Memory Verse, Prayer Focus, Bible Goals. Use this space to record, remind, and remember these weekly focuses and desired growth plans.

5.   To Do List. Because time is precious, use this space to record the most important things you need to get done this week. Anything else you complete is a bonus—icing on the cake!

6.   Letters, Calls, Connections. Who are the people you need to connect with, encounter, and encourage this week? Take time to ask God if your list is complete.

B.Y.O.B. and Hybrid Approaches:

If keeping your week scheduled in a daily planner or smart phone works better for you, great! Adapt as needed. The important thing is to include these components and reminders in your weekly plan.

My Weekly Overview

Week of: _____

Verse of the week:

Daily Time with God:

Mon	Tue	Wed	Thu	Fri	Sat	Sun

Memory Verse:

Prayer Focus:

Bible Reading & Study Goals:

To Do List:

_____ ☐ _____ ☐
_____ ☐ _____ ☐
_____ ☐ _____ ☐
_____ ☐ _____ ☐

Letters/Calls/Emails/Connections:

_____ ☐ _____ ☐
_____ ☐ _____ ☐
_____ ☐ _____ ☐

my spiritual journal

Have you ever just needed a safe place to put your thoughts and feelings? If you are human, the answer most likely is "yes!" Too many people, Christians included, choose *not* to share their inner musings and ponderings for fear of being judged, dismissed, lectured, or fixed.

Good news for those in need of a safe place with someone safe who will listen! David, the shepherd, king, and poet in the Bible, proclaims of God, *"You are my hiding place; You will protect me from trouble and surround me with songs of deliverance"* (Psalm 32:7).

David knew a lot about needing a trusted friend in a safe setting. He was on the run a lot from harmful people and circumstances. The safest place he knew was in God's presence. There, David felt protected, sung over, cared for.

A great place to pour out your heart in a safe environment is in your spiritual journal. God will sit with you as you write your deepest feelings, hardest questions, biggest frustrations, and most troubling confessions.

While a spiritual journal is a great place to express your struggles and hardships, it is equally the place to praise God and celebrate all that is right and good about God and life. And, it gives you an invaluable space to dialogue with God, process all you encounter on a day-to-day basis, and record all that God is teaching you in life.

The instructions for My Spiritual Journal are simple:

1. Fill in the date.

2. Open your heart and move your pen. Be honest with God and yourself. Allow what is in you to make its way to pen and paper. Trust that God is your safest Listener and most trusted Friend, who sings songs of delight over you (Zephaniah 3:17).

3. Consider one or more questions for reflection. Ask God and see if He prompts you to contemplate any specific questions with Him such as:

- What are You teaching me today, God?
- How did today go, Lord? Where did I do well, and where have I missed it?
- How did that conversation go?
- How can I better reflect You in that next time, Lord?
- What were my true motives with that?
- What strengths do you see in me, and how do you want to develop them?
- What weaknesses do You see in me, and how do you want to meet me in them?
- What victories and successes can we celebrate today?
- What was important here that I need to remember?
- Is my time and energy being spent in the right places?
- How can I partner with what You are doing?
- Am I seeing, stopping, and spending time with You and others?
- Along with obeying you today, Lord, did I also *enjoy* You?

My Spiritual Journal

Date: _____

Journal Entry:

Date: _____

Journal Entry:

my life-changing experiences

The benefit and reward of watching God work in your life is well worth the time it takes to write it down. And the process is easy! As you do so, you will join the Psalm-writer in saying, *"Praise the Lord, my soul, and forget not all His benefits"* (Psalm 103:2).

1.   Fill in the date and location. This helps you track your growth from week to week, month to month, year to year. Noting the location will also help you remember and visualize the details in the future. Over time, you will see how far you have come, and how faithful the Lord has been.

2.   Describe the life-changing experience. Write down the experience, decision, or commitment in a short statement. Don't worry too much about what should or should not be recorded or how to word it. This acts as your memory list, and you can include anything that is significant to you. You will be grateful that you made the time to track your walk with God.

3.   Review and recommit. If your experience was important to you two weeks or two months ago, it should still be important to you today. Periodically take time to review these experiences and thank God for the work He is doing in your life. Affirm the spiritual growth decisions you have made, recommit to live them out, and seek to share them with those God brings into your life to encourage in their faith!

My Life-Changing Experiences

Date: _____   Location: _____

Life-Changing Experience:

Date: _____   Location: _____

Life-Changing Experience:

further resources on reflection

Capture the QR Code below to access the Spiritual Life Notebook resource page or go to: www.ForgeForward.org/SLN.

You will find:

- Printable My Weekly Overview, My Spiritual Journal, and My Life-Changing Experiences journal pages.
- A free download of the resource "Ways God Speaks to Us" from the Forge *Life on Purpose* course. Discover how God has commissioned you to impact others in their everyday lives as you listen to Him!

up-close in kingdom investment

. . .

engaging kingdom investment as a lifestyle

"Freely you have received," Jesus said, *"freely give"* (Matthew 10:8). When you have been well-loved, you want to love well. When you have been forgiven much, you want to forgive much. And when you have been blessed, you want to be a blessing—with everything you have, with all that you are.

All we have comes from God. When we commit our lives to God, He doesn't own part of who we are and what we have. As Master and Lord of our lives, He owns it all. The truth is, believer or not, God owns everything everywhere. It is just when we submit our lives to His lordship that we discover and recognize that all we have and own is simply on loan from God.

That is why we invest in what matters most to God: people and His Kingdom. When we love God, giving and investing in things that matter to Him become so much more than fulfilling a religious obligation, appeasing God, or forking over our fair share to God so we can have and control the rest. Far from it! When we love God, what matters to Him matters more and more to us. And investing in things that matter to God moves from being a chore and drag to something joyful, meaningful, and delightful!

Since all we have belongs to God, every person, every situation, every Kingdom project and plan provides opportunity to put God's resources (on loan to us) into action! Our mindset and decision-making become a part of our Kingdom investment lifestyle as we daily walk with God, putting time, energy, and resources into the people and plans He guides us toward.

Do you remember the earlier section on prayer, specifically the "Yield" section where Jesus taught us to pray, *"**Your** Kingdom come. **Your** will be done—on earth as it is in heaven"*? This is the Kingdom we are investing in. God's Kingdom is wherever His rule and reign are the reality. It is the place where God's as-it-should-be love and character are present and active. Jesus talked a lot about the Kingdom of God. He often invited those He was near to be a part of what He was up to: filling hearts on earth with more of the heart of heaven.

And many joined him. People invested their time, opened their homes, sold their property, donated their possessions, fed strangers, cared for widows, trained others in the faith, traveled at their own expense to share the Good News of Jesus, used their skills and energy to invest in helping God's Kingdom expand, and so much more!

Like the boy who offered to Jesus his sack lunch consisting of five loaves and two fish, the offering that many contribute to God's Kingdom may not seem like much. But if, like the boy, they offer all they have, that is enough. Jesus can use any willing investment to feed multitudes! And Jesus will do the same with what you offer. Imagine what God can do with the resources, time, and energy you invest in His Kingdom with all you are and have!

Blessed to be a Blessing

"It is more blessed to give than to receive." (Acts 20:35). We quote this verse a lot. But we don't always act like we believe it. It is really true, though. We receive some of our greatest blessings in life when we give of our finances, time, and energy for the sake of others.

This section of your *Spiritual Life Notebook* is designed to help you give more—and experience even greater blessings as you do. It provides a place for you to record the Kingdom investments you make in people's lives and God's Kingdom as you give of yourself and your resources.

Abraham, who the Bible calls "The Father of Nations," was greatly blessed by God for one purpose: to be a blessing to many. Abraham's investments blessed generations. His concern was not to give God a little and make sure his children and grandchildren benefited. His desire was to live in such faithful obedience to God and generosity toward others that his great, great, great, great descendants would be blessed by the blessing He received from God. That means Abraham invested in Kingdom things for people he would never meet or know.

You and I are recipients of Abraham's blessing. Let's bless others as God continues to bless us. We have been blessed to be a blessing. Let's do it on a daily basis.

kingdom investment tips

1. Your investment is primarily about others. For those who invest their money financially or their minds educationally or their bodies athletically—the investment and payoff is often to benefit and pay dividends for oneself. And those kinds of investments are great! Kingdom investments, however, are not primarily about us and what we get. They are about pleasing God, spiritually benefiting others, and advancing God's Kingdom. While we are often blessed having invested in God's Kingdom, it's never our motive to give to personally get. The reward of investing is pleasing God and impacting others.

2. Investments take time. Investing in a garden takes time. As does investing in the stock market (day trading aside), investing in a music career, or investing in a relationship. Investing in people and God's Kingdom often take time as well. "I gave and nothing happened," or "I spent time with them, and I see no change," is not the language of investment. The Apostle Paul was quick to point out that our task in investing is to "*plant and water*," it is God who does the growing (I Corinthians 3:6). You will do well if you faithfully invest what you have and who you are and leave the results with God. God never wastes anything. He will take good care of all you invest.

3. Investments require sacrifice. Perhaps you have heard the phrase, "If it was that easy, everybody would do it!" Investing in people and God's Kingdom is not easy! Perhaps that is why "*the laborers are few*" in reaping a Kingdom harvest (Matthew 9:37). People require time, energy, patience, perseverance, and so much more. Investing our money, surrendering our calendars, and volunteering our skills for Kingdom causes is not always comfortable or effortless.

But what we do as Kingdom investors, we do for love. One of the greatest examples of such love in the Bible is when a woman of little financial means breaks open a very expensive jar of perfume—all for love of Jesus (read the whole story in Luke 7:36-50). Here is the point: Investing in others often requires sacrificing things most would keep for themselves. That is the beauty of investing Kingdom-style. It is really an investment of love. Jesus, out of His great love, invested in us sacrificially (Philippians 2:6-11). Jesus asks us to *"have the same mindset"* (Philippians 2:2) and do likewise (I John 4:19).

4. Know the source of your resources. We already addressed this, but it bears repeating. Your stuff doesn't belong to you. Say it with me, "My stuff is not my stuff!" If we hold our possessions, our time, our life with open hands—knowing that they are simply things for us to steward or care for—it is much easier to give what we have and who we are freely to God and others.

It is when we clench our lives and things with closed fists (as if it all belongs to us) that we run into trouble and become *self*-centered when it comes to God, His Kingdom, and others. You have a very well-to-do Father. He is wealthy in every aspect of the word. He has already blessed you beyond measure. You can rest assured that your Father— who not only "has the whole world in His hands" but also made the world He holds—will give you all you need and fulfill you as you bless others with things He has blessed you with.

5. Live free of clutter, baggage, and debt. Far too many people want to give—if they could. But they can't. They can't give financially because they are so strapped in debt, there is nothing left to give at the end of all their bills. Others spend so much time maintaining all their toys and possessions, they have no time to invest anywhere else. Yet others clutter their lives with busyness and schedules and personal needs. They simply do not have the energy to invest in other people. To say it simply: Live as simply as possible. Live within your means, be spiritually and emotionally healthy, and do not let the accumulation of things prevent you from investing in what matters most.

B.Y.O.B. and Hybrid Approaches:

As with the other sections, blend what is here with what you already do and what will work best for you. Use methods, apps, notebooks you already have in place. The goal is Kingdom investment, not record-keeping frustration!

people as kingdom investment

Jesus' number one priority and the greatest use of His time and energy was investing in people. We invest in things we care about and love. Jesus once told a group of followers that it is our treasures (our time, resources, thoughts, and energy) that actually tell us where our heart is (Matthew 6:21). It is not our lips but our active investment of time, resources, and energy that expose what we care about and love. For Jesus, it was people. As His followers, people are our treasured investment too.

my ministry of encouragement

One great (also fun and easy!) way to invest in God's kingdom is to be an encourager. Hebrews 3:13 says, *"Encourage one another daily, as long as it is called 'Today,' so that none of you may be hardened by sin's deceitfulness."*

The word "encourage" literally means "to empower with courage." Have you noticed what happens when someone encourages you? All of a sudden, you feel a resurgence of energy and you experience new faith and courage to face the hardships in your life. Encouragement persuades you to keep moving forward and it reinforces God's vision for who you can become!

Encouragement is extremely simple yet infinitely powerful. Imagine what would happen if every Kingdom-laboring, Christ-follower constantly encouraged one another! The burst of increased courage and energy would change not only them but their world.

We all can get discouraged and lose sight of God's everyday work in us and through us. Encouraging notes, phone calls, and emails can inspire us to keep fighting the good fight.

Your words impact people more than you will ever know. They carry the potential to send massive ripples beyond anything you could ever imagine. Kingdom advances are greater wherever the efforts are greater, and the efforts are greater wherever courage is greater, and courage is greater wherever the *encouragers* are at work!

So, practice encouraging people any and every way you can. Get creative. Be observant and let people know how wonderfully God made them, what God sees in them, and how they are loved by God and many!

1. Fill in the name of the recipient. This helps you track the depth and breadth of God's encouragement through you over time. Notice if He is consistently focusing you on the same people over and over or if He is sending you to different people each time.

2. Describe the type of encouragement. When you observe the work God is doing in people's lives, tell them. When people bless you, thank them. When you see people trying to improve their lives, affirm them. When you see people persevering in the midst of difficult circumstances, encourage them. Through handwritten notes, emails, brief encouraging text messages, conversations, phone calls, voicemails, prayer emails, and gifts, you can build people up. You might consider purchasing print and digital spiritual resources to bless people in their journey. There are so many ways to reach out and "encourage one another daily" as Scripture admonishes us.

3. Note the date. This will help you refer back and review your encouragement list from time to time. If your encouragement seemed to make a difference in someone's life, make sure to note it—it will provide more fuel for you to continue a lifestyle of encouragement.

NOTE: Many of the encouraging written notes you give will likely be saved and reread again and again. Written notes are highly impactful! While written notes may be one of the most impactful forms of encouragement, your encouraging gifts, texts, and voicemails will likely have a strong impact too because people tend to save and revisit whatever blesses and encourages them.

"Therefore, encourage one another and build each other up, just as in fact you are doing." - I Thessalonians 5:11

My Ministry of Encouragement		
Name	Type of Encouragement	Date

my baton passing relationships

Jesus implemented an exponential growth strategy more than two thousand years ago. While He preached to countless people, He spent the majority of His time with twelve men. He sought to grow these ordinary guys into passionate, everyday Kingdom Laborers who would love God and others. By investing Himself in their lives, He taught them to likewise invest themselves in others. And so on.

Jesus' spiritual multiplication plan simply involves passing your spiritual wealth—special scriptural passages and spiritual growth resources that have been helpful to you, gained wisdom and understanding that has come to you from your developing walk with God—to others who in turn will do the same for others.

That is what Jesus did. He shared with His disciples what He had received from His Father. So following the example of His Father, He loved and cared for them. He taught them about the ways of God and building His Kingdom. Then Jesus challenged them to go out and pour themselves into others the way He had poured into them.

The long-term success of Jesus' approach proved that spending more time with fewer people results in deeper life-impact, and over time ultimately yields greater results for the Kingdom.

Many people are intimidated by the idea of coaching, helping, or mentoring someone. They assume that God requires perfection in order to use us. But God simply wants us to re-invest in others whatever He has given to us. By taking an inventory of anything that has helped you grow closer to God—you will understand what God has prepared in advance for you to offer others (see Ephesians 2:10).

God has given you spiritual insights to share. He is unfolding a unique testimony of His love and faithfulness in your life, in part so you can bless others. He will pour out through your life what He wants to see passed on into the hearts and lives of others.

Just give out of the overflow of what God has given you.

God will lead you to people He wants you to help and encourage. He will work through you to raise up strongly committed followers who will also reach out and help others with the same kind of help they have received from you.

"Therefore go and MAKE DISCIPLES . . ." (Matthew 28:19). A Disciple is "a perpetual learner," one who is deeply committed to growing spiritually, applying God's Word to daily living and obeying the counsel and direction of the Holy Spirit. Ultimately, a Baton Passer is one who reproduces other disciples.

The My Baton Passing Relationships pages in this section will help you keep track of the people God is enabling you to invest in:

1. Fill in the name, address, phone, email, and social media contact information of the person you are discipling. This will help you keep in touch with them and naturally become a part of their life. You will likely want to reach out to them periodically with encouragement and to let them know you are praying for them.

2. Note their birthday and any other important dates. Remembering a birthday or anniversary can be a powerful way to show that you care about the person you are discipling, their family, and their journey.

3. Note the dates you began meeting and when the person you are mentoring begins to mentor another. Noting these dates will let you see the process of multiplication at work!

4. Record observations of initial need, scriptures or materials given, and spiritual progress. Writing down insights of needs from the Holy Spirit is crucial as you mentor another. Ultimately, God is using you to mature and grow this person, so it follows that the most important key will be your sensitivity to let God lead you. Taking the time to jot down topics discussed and resources used will also help you remain focused and intentional as you refer back and review progress.

5. Plan further contact or follow-up. Use this space to set the time for your next meeting or take some notes for future study and conversation.

My Baton Passing Relationships
Name:
Address:
Phone:
Email: *Social Media:*
Important Dates (birthday, anniversary, etc.)
Date began meeting:
Areas of initial need:
Scriptures or spiritual growth materials used or given:
Observations:
Spiritual progress:
Date she or he began mentoring another:
Further contact or follow-up:

my multiplying movements

When it comes to God's Kingdom, addition is good, but multiplication is what we are aiming for—and your baton-passing relationships are great opportunities for Kingdom multiplication!

If you ever studied compound interest in school or experienced the reward of watching compound interest increase in a savings account (or the not-so-good side of compound interest on a loan), you know how powerful multiplication can be.

Let's say you spiritually invest your time and energy into five people. And praise the Lord, amazingly, they each respond to the Gospel. Now, five more believers are a part of God's Kingdom. Let's say you repeat the scenario over the next four years. You know the math—20 more believers *added* to God's Kingdom. How wonderful! And indeed it is.

Let's see what multiplication can do. What if the first five people you invested in that first year turned around and invested into five others? Assuming the same percent of people responded, the second year 30 new believers would be the result of those spiritual investments. Repeating the same scenario the third, then fourth year, 780 people would know the joy of knowing Jesus and the life He brings. That is the power of Kingdom multiplication through intentional baton-passing!

We want to be Kingdom multipliers! That means we want to invest in others who will in turn invest in others. And, we want to invest in those people and places who are about the business of Kingdom multi-plication.

You do not need to be a seasoned Christian to be a Kingdom Multi-plier. You simply need to love God and others authentically, willingly share your stories of how God has shown up in your life, and invite others to do the same.

Begin investing today in the lives of others who will invest in others. The quicker you begin, the faster God's Kingdom will advance. One of the easiest ways you can do this is by joining and then starting a *Multiplying Movements* group. The team at Forge has created all the resources you will need to walk you through each step of the process.

Check out MultiplyingMovements.com to begin. *Multiplying Movements* is not simply one-time material, but a discipleship tool designed for you to lead others through, to make disciples, and for them to in turn lead others through, so that the movement multiplies far beyond you as an individual!

Here is how you can use the My Multiplying Movements form:

1. **Track your steps toward launching your *Multiplying Movements* group**. These steps have been designed with intentionality and years of experience behind them to serve you in launching your *Multiplying Movements* group as you go through the process. Use this page to track the status of your multiplication and know that it can be repeated over and over again with new groups of people.

2. **Note the names of people God might be highlighting to be part of your group.** Ask God to show you who He has picked out to do *Multiplying Movements* with you. It might be just one person or it could be a group of up to about 20. Let God put the group together—just make sure you are listening and being obedient to His promptings! Pray for your group prospects regularly.

3. **Note the names of people you are praying for and sharing Jesus with.** Ask God to show you where He wants you to invest in prayer and how you can reveal His heart to these people continually. You may find that some people start in this section and then move to the *Multiplying Movements* group section, or vice versa.

My Multiplying Movements	
Date Completed	*Phases To Launch My Multiplying Movements Group*
	1. Complete *Multiplying Movements* myself.
	2. Practice seeing, stopping, and spending time with people.
	3. List and pray for people God might want me to take through *Multiplying Movements.*
	4. Ask them to consider/pray about meeting together.
	5. Confirm where and when we will meet.
	6. Keep praying and remind group of meeting details.
	7. Launch my group and connect with Forge for support.
	8. As you near the end, encourage your members to launch and begin their own *Multiplying Movements* groups!
Date	*People God may want me to take through Multiplying Movements:*
Date	*People I am intentionally praying for and sharing Jesus with:*

my financial giving

Whatever your income, God can accomplish great things through your financial giving because He uses the *temporal* money of His people to do His *eternal* work. So anything you do in partnership with Him lasts forever.

Your tithes and offerings are investments that help churches and ministries reach and serve people spiritually, emotionally, and physically. "Tithing" is usually defined as 10% of a person's gross income, while "offerings" are considered any monetary gift over and above the tithe.

Do you think of them as investments?

The ROI (return on investment) plays an important role in how people invest their money in the stock market. Your investment into God's Kingdom work brings an *eternal* ROI because His Kingdom lasts forever. Think about it: Your gifts create a ripple effect that resonates for eternity!

In order to lessen the risk, people who invest in the stock market also place a high priority on diversifying their portfolio. In the same way, you may want to diversify your portfolio when investing in God's Kingdom. For instance, in addition to investing in your *local* church, you may also want to invest in *international* missions. In addition to investing in ministries that strengthen disciples in their walk with Christ, you may also want to invest in evangelistic ministries.

In addition to investing in the needs of the poor, elderly, widows, and orphans, you may also want to invest in ministries raising up new generations of Kingdom laborers—which is the ultimate heartbeat of Forge and is happening globally through: evangelistic outreach and traveling speakers, practical equipping, and discipleship resources, all fueling Jesus' everyday everywhere movement (ForgeForward.org).

Unlike investing in the stock market, however, diversifying your giving in God's Kingdom is not about reducing risk. It is about impacting a variety of people in different ways while advancing God's Kingdom!

People interpret Scripture differently when they consider where and how much they should give. Regardless, the Bible clearly tells us that God wants us to give generously—and cheerfully! His Word says that *"God loves a cheerful giver"* (2 Corinthians 9:7). So, as you seek to *"find out what pleases the Lord"* (Ephesians 5:10), know that however He wants you to invest your life, finances, time, and resources—He loves it when you do so with joyful energy!

Enjoy using this section to record your financial investments in God's Kingdom:

1. Fill in the date of your gifts, the amount of total income you are giving from, and the amounts you give to various churches and ministries. Recording both your income and your gifts will let you see how much of your income you are tithing and offering. Take special care to note the recipients of your gifts so you can look back at them over time and even track for tax purposes.

2. Complete the "Blessings/Notes" area. Record the reason you gave the gift and return later to record any known blessings that resulted from your gift. Watch and see God work through your gifts!

My Financial Giving	
Date:	*Income: $*
Local Church	$
Missions & Outreach	$
	$
	$
	$
TOTAL Given	$

Blessings/Notes:

My Financial Giving	
Date:	*Income: $*
Local Church	$
Missions & Outreach	$
	$
	$
	$
TCTAL Given	$

Blessings/Notes:

my recommended reading

Talk to any great person, and you will find out that they have read some great books. In fact, maybe you should do just that. Find out what some of the most meaningful books are that your spiritual mentors, friends, and others have read!

There has probably never been such an incredible amount of resources available to Christians who really want to learn and grow. However, never, and maybe it is worth repeating, never should the Bible be put aside or pre-empted. It should always be first on your reading list.

But there are books and booklets that are real life-changers that you can read in addition to God's Word. Use this section to record books that will further sharpen your life, so you don't lose track of them:

1. Fill in the title and author. Keeping this list will help you not forget when a great book comes up in conversation or life.

2. Note the date started and finished. This will help you see what books you are reading and have finished recently. When you finish a book, you may also find this list helpful to remind you of good books you can share with others.

My Recommended Reading / Books			
Title	Author	Date Started	Date Finished

further resources on kingdom investment

Capture the QR Code below to access the Spiritual Life Notebook
resource page or go to: www.ForgeForward.org/SLN.

You will find:

- Printable My Ministry of Encouragement, My Baton Passing
  Relationships, My Multiplying Movements, My Financial
  Giving, and My Recommended Reading journal pages.
- Link to a short booklet entitled, *"Baton Passing Relationships"*
  (available at ForgeForward.org/Resources).
- A free download of the *Multiplying Movements* video resource
  on the Forge App. *Multiplying Movements* is not simply one-
  time material, but a discipleship tool designed for you to lead
  others through, to make disciples, and for them to in turn lead
  others through, so that the movement multiplies far beyond
  you as an individual!

my spiritual life notebook

60-Day Supply of Pages

The remaining pages of this book are a 60-day supply of *Spiritual Life Notebook* journal pages for your convenience. If it makes it easier for you to begin and establish healthy spiritual habits, we consider these pages well worth it! You can print more as needed when these are full, or purchase a bound, blank *Spiritual Life Notebook* at ForgeForward. org/resources.

If you would prefer to start your own notebook and create journal pages or ways of engaging God's Word, prayer, reflection, and Kingdom investment—equally phenomenal!

Our goal is not to make you some sort of super-devo doer. We want you up-close to Jesus, the One who knows you best and will best guide your life into His Kingdom purposes.

Enjoy the journey! Your maturing as a follower of Jesus continues day-by-day, right now!

my bible study

. . .

My Bible Study

Scripture Passage: _____ Date: _____

1. **HEAD: What is this passage saying?** What is the main message? What do I learn about God—the Father, Jesus, the Holy Spirit—or people, creation, evil, etc.?

2. **HEART: What is God speaking to me, or how did this impact me personally?** What part sticks out to me? What changes do I need to make in my beliefs, attitudes, actions?

3. **HANDS: This very week, how will I practically obey what God has shown me?** What next step will I take?

4. **FEET: Who will I share with?** Is there anyone in my life that I need to tell about what I learned to encourage them?

_____

_____

_____

_____

_____

_____

_____

_____

_____

_____

_____

_____

Question(s) to ask my spiritual mentor regarding this:

_____

_____

_____

_____

_____

Verses to memorize:

_____

_____

My Bible Study

Scripture Passage: _____ Date: _____

1. **HEAD: What is this passage saying?** What is the main message? What do I learn about God—the Father, Jesus, the Holy Spirit—or people, creation, evil, etc.?

2. **HEART: What is God speaking to me, or how did this impact me personally?** What part sticks out to me? What changes do I need to make in my beliefs, attitudes, actions?

3. **HANDS: This very week, how will I practically obey what God has shown me?** What next step will I take?

4. **FEET: Who will I share with?** Is there anyone in my life that I need to tell about what I learned to encourage them?

_____
_____
_____
_____
_____
_____
_____
_____
_____
_____
_____
_____
_____

Question(s) to ask my spiritual mentor regarding this:

_____
_____
_____
_____
_____

Verses to memorize:

_____
_____

My Bible Study

Scripture Passage: _____ Date: _____

1. **HEAD: What is this passage saying?** What is the main message? What do I learn about God—the Father, Jesus, the Holy Spirit—or people, creation, evil, etc.?

2. **HEART: What is God speaking to me, or how did this impact me personally?** What part sticks out to me? What changes do I need to make in my beliefs, attitudes, actions?

3. **HANDS: This very week, how will I practically obey what God has shown me?** What next step will I take?

4. **FEET: Who will I share with?** Is there anyone in my life that I need to tell about what I learned to encourage them?

_____

_____

_____

_____

_____

_____

_____

_____

_____

_____

_____

_____

Question(s) to ask my spiritual mentor regarding this:

_____

_____

_____

_____

_____

Verses to memorize:

_____

_____

My Bible Study

Scripture Passage: _____ Date: _____

1. **HEAD: What is this passage saying?** What is the main message? What do I learn about God—the Father, Jesus, the Holy Spirit—or people, creation, evil, etc.?

2. **HEART: What is God speaking to me, or how did this impact me personally?** What part sticks out to me? What changes do I need to make in my beliefs, attitudes, actions?

3. **HANDS: This very week, how will I practically obey what God has shown me?** What next step will I take?

4. **FEET: Who will I share with?** Is there anyone in my life that I need to tell about what I learned to encourage them?

_____

_____

_____

_____

_____

_____

_____

_____

_____

_____

_____

_____

Question(s) to ask my spiritual mentor regarding this:

_____

_____

_____

_____

Verses to memorize:

_____

_____

My Bible Study

Scripture Passage: _____ Date: _____

1. **HEAD: What is this passage saying?** What is the main message? What do I learn about God—the Father, Jesus, the Holy Spirit—or people, creation, evil, etc.?

2. **HEART: What is God speaking to me, or how did this impact me personally?** What part sticks out to me? What changes do I need to make in my beliefs, attitudes, actions?

3. **HANDS: This very week, how will I practically obey what God has shown me?** What next step will I take?

4. **FEET: Who will I share with?** Is there anyone in my life that I need to tell about what I learned to encourage them?

_____

_____

_____

_____

_____

_____

_____

_____

_____

_____

_____

_____

Question(s) to ask my spiritual mentor regarding this:

_____

_____

_____

_____

_____

Verses to memorize:

_____

_____

My Bible Study

Scripture Passage: _____ Date: _____

1. **HEAD: What is this passage say ng?** What is the main message? What do I learn about God—the Father, Jesus, the Holy Spirit—or people, creation, evil, etc.?

2. **HEART: What is God speaking to me, or how did this impact me personally?** What part sticks out to me? What changes do I need to make in my beliefs, attitudes, actions?

3. **HANDS: This very week, how will I practically obey what God has shown me?** What next step will I take?

4. **FEET: Who will I share with?** Is there anyone in my life that I need to tell about what I learned to encourage them?

_____
_____
_____
_____
_____
_____
_____
_____
_____
_____
_____
_____
_____

Question(s) to ask my spiritual mentor regarding this:

_____
_____
_____
_____
_____

Verses to memorize:

_____
_____

My Bible Study

Scripture Passage: _____ Date: _____

1. **HEAD: What is this passage saying?** What is the main message? What do I learn about God—the Father, Jesus, the Holy Spirit—or people, creation, evil, etc.?

2. **HEART: What is God speaking to me, or how did this impact me personally?** What part sticks out to me? What changes do I need to make in my beliefs, attitudes, actions?

3. **HANDS: This very week, how will I practically obey what God has shown me?** What next step will I take?

4. **FEET: Who will I share with?** Is there anyone in my life that I need to tell about what I learned to encourage them?

_____

_____

_____

_____

_____

_____

_____

_____

_____

_____

_____

_____

Question(s) to ask my spiritual mentor regarding this:

_____

_____

_____

_____

_____

Verses to memorize:

_____

_____

My Bible Study

Scripture Passage: _____ Date: _____

1. **HEAD: What is this passage saying?** What is the main message? What do I learn about God—the Father, Jesus, the Holy Spirit—or people, creation, evil, etc.?

2. **HEART: What is God speaking to me, or how did this impact me personally?** What part sticks out to me? What changes do I need to make in my beliefs, attitudes, actions?

3. **HANDS: This very week, how will I practically obey what God has shown me?** What next step will I take?

4. **FEET: Who will I share with?** Is there anyone in my life that I need to tell about what I learned to encourage them?

_____
_____
_____
_____
_____
_____
_____
_____
_____
_____
_____
_____

Question(s) to ask my spiritual mentor regarding this:

_____
_____
_____
_____

Verses to memorize:

_____
_____

My Bible Study

Scripture Passage: _____ Date: _____

1. **HEAD: What is this passage saying?** What is the main message? What do I learn about God—the Father, Jesus, the Holy Spirit—or people, creation, evil, etc.?

2. **HEART: What is God speaking to me, or how did this impact me personally?** What part sticks out to me? What changes do I need to make in my beliefs, attitudes, actions?

3. **HANDS: This very week, how will I practically obey what God has shown me?** What next step will I take?

4. **FEET: Who will I share with?** Is there anyone in my life that I need to tell about what I learned to encourage them?

_____
_____
_____
_____
_____
_____
_____
_____
_____
_____
_____
_____
_____

Question(s) to ask my spiritual mentor regarding this:

_____
_____
_____
_____
_____

Verses to memorize:

_____
_____

My Bible Study

Scripture Passage: _____ Date: _____

1. **HEAD: What is this passage saying?** What is the main message? What do I learn about God—the Father, Jesus, the Holy Spirit—or people, creation, evil, etc.?

2. **HEART: What is God speaking to me, or how did this impact me personally?** What part sticks out to me? What changes do I need to make in my beliefs, attitudes, actions?

3. **HANDS: This very week, how will I practically obey what God has shown me?** What next step will I take?

4. **FEET: Who will I share with?** Is there anyone in my life that I need to tell about what I learned to encourage them?

_____

_____

_____

_____

_____

_____

_____

_____

_____

_____

_____

_____

Question(s) to ask my spiritual mentor regarding this:

_____

_____

_____

_____

Verses to memorize:

_____

_____

My Bible Study

Scripture Passage: _____ Date: _____

1. **HEAD: What is this passage saying?** What is the main message? What do I learn about God—the Father, Jesus, the Holy Spirit—or people, creation, evil, etc.?

2. **HEART: What is God speaking to me, or how did this impact me personally?** What part sticks out to me? What changes do I need to make in my beliefs, attitudes, actions?

3. **HANDS: This very week, how will I practically obey what God has shown me?** What next step will I take?

4. **FEET: Who will I share with?** Is there anyone in my life that I need to tell about what I learned to encourage them?

_____
_____
_____
_____
_____
_____
_____
_____
_____
_____
_____
_____

Question(s) to ask my spiritual mentor regarding this:

_____
_____
_____
_____
_____

Verses to memorize:

_____
_____

My Bible Study

Scripture Passage: _____ Date: _____

1. **HEAD: What is this passage say ng?** What is the main message? What do I learn about God—the Father, Jesus, the Holy Spirit—or people, creation, evil, etc.?

2. **HEART: What is God speaking to me, or how did this impact me personally?** What part sticks out to me? What changes do I need to make in my beliefs, attitudes, actions?

3. **HANDS: This very week, how will I practically obey what God has shown me?** What next step will I take?

4. **FEET: Who will I share with?** Is there anyone in my life that I need to tell about what I learned to encourage them?

_____

_____

_____

_____

_____

_____

_____

_____

_____

_____

_____

_____

Question(s) to ask my spiritual mentor regarding this:

_____

_____

_____

_____

Verses to memorize:

_____

_____

My Bible Study

Scripture Passage: _____ Date: _____

1. **HEAD: What is this passage saying?** What is the main message? What do I learn about God—the Father, Jesus, the Holy Spirit—or people, creation, evil, etc.?

2. **HEART: What is God speaking to me, or how did this impact me personally?** What part sticks out to me? What changes do I need to make in my beliefs, attitudes, actions?

3. **HANDS: This very week, how will I practically obey what God has shown me?** What next step will I take?

4. **FEET: Who will I share with?** Is there anyone in my life that I need to tell about what I learned to encourage them?

_____

_____

_____

_____

_____

_____

_____

_____

_____

_____

_____

_____

Question(s) to ask my spiritual mentor regarding this:

_____

_____

_____

_____

Verses to memorize:

_____

_____

My Bible Study

Scripture Passage: _____ Date: _____

1. **HEAD: What is this passage saying?** What is the main message? What do I learn about God—the Father, Jesus, the Holy Spirit—or people, creation, evil, etc.?

2. **HEART: What is God speaking to me, or how did this impact me personally?** What part sticks out to me? What changes do I need to make in my beliefs, attitudes, actions?

3. **HANDS: This very week, how will I practically obey what God has shown me?** What next step will I take?

4. **FEET: Who will I share with?** Is there anyone in my life that I need to tell about what I learned to encourage them?

_____

_____

_____

_____

_____

_____

_____

_____

_____

_____

_____

_____

_____

Question(s) to ask my spiritual mentor regarding this:

_____

_____

_____

_____

Verses to memorize:

_____

_____

My Bible Study

Scripture Passage: _____ Date: _____

1. **HEAD: What is this passage saying?** What is the main message? What do I learn about God—the Father, Jesus, the Holy Spirit—or people, creation, evil, etc.?

2. **HEART: What is God speaking to me, or how did this impact me personally?** What part sticks out to me? What changes do I need to make in my beliefs, attitudes, actions?

3. **HANDS: This very week, how will I practically obey what God has shown me?** What next step will I take?

4. **FEET: Who will I share with?** Is there anyone in my life that I need to tell about what I learned to encourage them?

_____
_____
_____
_____
_____
_____
_____
_____
_____
_____
_____
_____

Question(s) to ask my spiritual mentor regarding this:

_____
_____
_____
_____
_____

Verses to memorize:

_____
_____

My Bible Study

Scripture Passage: _____ Date: _____

1. **HEAD: What is this passage saying?** What is the main message? What do I learn about God—the Father, Jesus, the Holy Spirit—or people, creation, evil, etc.?

2. **HEART: What is God speaking to me, or how did this impact me personally?** What part sticks out to me? What changes do I need to make in my beliefs, attitudes, actions?

3. **HANDS: This very week, how will I practically obey what God has shown me?** What next step will I take?

4. **FEET: Who will I share with?** Is there anyone in my life that I need to tell about what I learned to encourage them?

_____
_____
_____
_____
_____
_____
_____
_____
_____
_____
_____
_____
_____
_____

Question(s) to ask my spiritual mentor regarding this:

_____
_____
_____
_____
_____

Verses to memorize:

_____
_____

My Bible Study

Scripture Passage: _____ Date: _____

1. **HEAD: What is this passage saying?** What is the main message? What do I learn about God—the Father, Jesus, the Holy Spirit—or people, creation, evil, etc.?

2. **HEART: What is God speaking to me, or how did this impact me personally?** What part sticks out to me? What changes do I need to make in my beliefs, attitudes, actions?

3. **HANDS: This very week, how will I practically obey what God has shown me?** What next step will I take?

4. **FEET: Who will I share with?** Is there anyone in my life that I need to tell about what I learned to encourage them?

_____

_____

_____

_____

_____

_____

_____

_____

_____

_____

_____

_____

_____

Question(s) to ask my spiritual mentor regarding this:

_____

_____

_____

_____

_____

Verses to memorize:

_____

_____

my reading through the bible

. . .

Old Testament

	1	2	3	4	5	6	7	8	9	10	11	12	13	14	15	16	17	18
Genesis	1	2	3	4	5	6	7	8	9	10	11	12	13	14	15	16	17	18
	19	20	21	22	23	24	25	26	27	28	29	30	31	32	33	34	35	36
	39	40	41	42	43	44	45	46	47	48	49	50						
Exodus	1	2	3	4	5	6	7	8	9	10	11	12	13	14	15	16	17	18
	19	20	21	22	23	24	25	26	27	28	29	30	31	32	33	34	35	36
	39	40																
Leviticus	1	2	3	4	5	6	7	8	9	10	11	12	13	14	15	16	17	18
	19	20	21	22	23	24	25	26	27									
Numbers	1	2	3	4	5	6	7	8	9	10	11	12	13	14	15	16	17	18
	19	20	21	22	23	24	25	26	27	28	29	30	31	32	33	34	35	36
Deuteronomy	1	2	3	4	5	6	7	8	9	10	11	12	13	14	15	16	17	18
	19	20	21	22	23	24	25	26	27	28	29	30	31	32	33	34		
Joshua	1	2	3	4	5	6	7	8	9	10	11	12	13	14	15	16	17	18
	19	20	21	22	23	24												
Judges	1	2	3	4	5	6	7	8	9	10	11	12	13	14	15	16	17	18
	19	20	21															
Ruth	1	2	3	4														
1 Samuel	1	2	3	4	5	6	7	8	9	10	11	12	13	14	15	16	17	18
	19	20	21	22	23	24	25	26	27	28	29	30	31					
2 Samuel	1	2	3	4	5	6	7	8	9	10	11	12	13	14	15	16	17	18
	19	20	21	22	23	24												
1 Kings	1	2	3	4	5	6	7	8	9	10	11	12	13	14	15	16	17	18
	19	20	21	22														
2 Kings	1	2	3	4	5	6	7	8	9	10	11	12	13	14	15	16	17	18
	19	20	21	22	23	24	25											
1 Chronicles	1	2	3	4	5	6	7	8	9	10	11	12	13	14	15	16	17	18
	19	20	21	22	23	24	25	26	27	28	29							
2 Chronicles	1	2	3	4	5	6	7	8	9	10	11	12	13	14	15	16	17	18
	19	20	21	22	23	24	25	26	27	28	29	30	31	32	33	34	35	36
Ezra	1	2	3	4	5	6	7	8	9	10								
Nehemiah	1	2	3	4	5	6	7	8	9	10	11	12	13					
Esther	1	2	3	4	5	6	7	8	9	10								
Job	1	2	3	4	5	6	7	8	9	10	11	12	13	14	15	16	17	18
	19	20	21	22	23	24	25	26	27	28	29	30	31	32	33	34	35	36
	37	38	39	40	41	42												

Old Testament

Psalms	1	2	3	4	5	6	7	8	9	10	11	12	13	14	15	16	17	18
	19	20	21	22	23	24	25	26	27	28	29	30	31	32	33	34	35	36
	37	38	39	40	41	42	43	44	45	46	47	48	49	50	51	52	53	54
	55	56	57	58	59	60	61	62	63	64	65	66	67	68	69	70	71	72
	73	74	75	76	77	78	79	80	81	82	83	84	85	86	87	88	89	90
	91	92	93	94	95	96	97	98	99	100	101	102	103	104	105	106	107	108
	109	110	111	112	113	114	115	116	117	118	119	120	121	122	123	124	125	126
	127	128	129	130	131	132	133	134	135	136	137	138	139	140	141	142	143	144
	145	146	147	148	149	150												
Proverbs	1	2	3	4	5	6	7	8	9	10	11	12	13	14	15	16	17	18
	19	20	21	22	23	24	25	26	27	28	29	30	31					
Ecclesiastes	1	2	3	4	5	6	7	8	9	10	11	12						
Song of Songs	1	2	3	4	5	6	7	8										
Isaiah	1	2	3	4	5	6	7	8	9	10	11	12	13	14	15	16	17	18
	19	20	21	22	23	24	25	26	27	28	29	30	31	32	33	34	35	36
	37	38	39	40	41	42	43	44	45	46	47	48	49	50	51	52	53	54
	55	56	57	58	59	60	61	62	63	64	65	66						
Jeremiah	1	2	3	4	5	6	7	8	9	10	11	12	13	14	15	16	17	18
	19	20	21	22	23	24	25	26	27	28	29	30	31	32	33	34	35	36
	37	38	39	40	41	42	43	44	45	46	47	48	49	50	51	52		
Lamentations	1	2	3	4	5													
Ezekiel	1	2	3	4	5	6	7	8	9	10	11	12	13	14	15	16	17	18
	19	20	21	22	23	24	25	26	27	28	29	30	31	32	33	34	35	36
	37	38	39	40	41	42	43	44	45	46	47	48						
Daniel	1	2	3	4	5	6	7	8	9	10	11	12						
Hosea	1	2	3	4	5	6	7	8	9	10	11	12	13	14				
Joel	1	2	3															
Amos	1	2	3	4	5	6	7	8	9									
Obadiah	1																	
Jonah	1	2	3	4														
Micah	1	2	3	4														
Nahum	1	2	3															
Habakkuk	1	2	3															
Zephaniah	1	2	3															
Haggai	1	2																
Zechariah	1	2	3	4	5	6	7	8	9	10	11	12	13	14				
Malachi	1	2	3	4														

New Testament

Matthew	1	2	3	4	5	6	7	8	9	10	11	12	13	14	15	16
	17	18	19	20	21	22	23	24	25	26	27	28	29	30		
Mark	1	2	3	4	5	6	7	8	9	10	11	12	13	14	15	16
Luke	1	2	3	4	5	6	7	8	9	10	11	12	13	14	15	16
	17	18	19	20	21	22	23	24								
John	1	2	3	4	5	6	7	8	9	10	11	12	13	14	15	16
	17	18	19	20	21											
Acts	1	2	3	4	5	6	7	8	9	10	11	12	13	14	15	16
		19	20	21	22	23	24	25	26	27	28					
Romans	1	2	3	4	5	6	7	8	9	10	11	12	13	14	15	16
1 Corinthians	1	2	3	4	5	6	7	8	9	10	11	12	13	14	15	16
2 Corinthians	1	2	3	4	5	6	7	8	9	10	11	12	13			
Galatians	1	2	3	4	5	6										
Ephesians	1	2	3	4	5	6										
Philippians	1	2	3	4												
Colossians	1	2	3	4												
1 Thessalonians	1	2	3	4												
2 Thessalonians	1	2	3													
1 Timothy	1	2	3	4	5	6										
2 Timothy	1	2	3	4												
Titus	1	2	3													
Philemon	1															
Hebrews	1	2	3	4	5	6	7	8	9	10	11					
James	1	2	3	4	5											
1 Peter	1	2	3	4	5											
2 Peter	1	2	3													
1 John	1	2	3	4	5											
2 John	1															
3 John	1															
Jude	1															
Revelation	1	2	3	4	5	6	7	8	9	10	11	12	13	14	15	16
	17	18	19	20	21	22										

my scripture memory

. . .

My Scripture Memory			
Scripture	Date Started	Date Memorized	Uses for This Verse

My Scripture Memory			
Scripture	Date Started	Date Memorized	Uses for This Verse

My Scripture Memory			
Scripture	Date Started	Date Memorized	Uses for This Verse

my sermon notes

. . .

My Sermon Notes

Speaker: _____   Text: _____

Date: _____   Topic: _____

_____
_____
_____
_____
_____
_____
_____
_____
_____
_____
_____
_____
_____
_____
_____

Summary *(In one sentence, the main thing God is saying to me through this sermon is . . .)*

_____
_____
_____
_____

Life Application *(The action steps I want to take are . . .)*

_____
_____
_____

My Sermon Notes

Speaker: _____   Text: _____

Date: _____   Topic: _____

_____
_____
_____
_____
_____
_____
_____
_____
_____
_____
_____
_____
_____
_____

Summary *(In one sentence, the main thing God is saying to me through this sermon is . . .)*

_____
_____
_____
_____
_____

Life Application *(The action steps I want to take are . . .)*

_____
_____
_____
_____

My Sermon Notes

Speaker: _____   Text: _____

Date: _____   Topic: _____

_____
_____
_____
_____
_____
_____
_____
_____
_____
_____
_____
_____
_____
_____
_____

Summary *(In one sentence, the main thing God is saying to me through this sermon is . . .)*

_____
_____
_____
_____
_____

Life Application *(The action steps I want to take are . . .)*

_____
_____
_____
_____

My Sermon Notes

Speaker: _____   Text: _____

Date: _____   Topic: _____

_____
_____
_____
_____
_____
_____
_____
_____
_____
_____
_____
_____
_____
_____
_____
_____
_____

Summary *(In one sentence, the main thing God is saying to me through this sermon is . . .)*

_____
_____
_____
_____
_____

Life Application *(The action steps I want to take are . . .)*

_____
_____
_____
_____

My Sermon Notes

Speaker: _____   Text: _____

Date: _____   Topic: _____

_____
_____
_____
_____
_____
_____
_____
_____
_____
_____
_____
_____
_____
_____
_____

Summary *(In one sentence, the main thing God is saying to me through this sermon is . . .)*

_____
_____
_____
_____
_____

Life Application *(The action steps I want to take are . . .)*

_____
_____
_____
_____

My Sermon Notes

Speaker: _____   Text: _____

Date: _____   Topic: _____

_____
_____
_____
_____
_____
_____
_____
_____
_____
_____
_____
_____
_____
_____
_____

Summary *(In one sentence, the main thing God is saying to me through this sermon is . . .)*

_____
_____
_____
_____
_____

Life Application *(The action steps I want to take are . . .)*

_____
_____
_____
_____

My Sermon Notes

Speaker: _____   Text: _____

Date: _____   Topic: _____

_____

_____

_____

_____

_____

_____

_____

_____

_____

_____

_____

_____

_____

_____

_____

_____

Summary *(In one sentence, the main thing God is saying to me through this sermon is . . .)*

_____

_____

_____

_____

Life Application *(The action steps I want to take are . . .)*

_____

_____

_____

_____

My Sermon Notes

Speaker: _____   Text: _____

Date: _____   Topic: _____

_____
_____
_____
_____
_____
_____
_____
_____
_____
_____
_____
_____
_____
_____
_____

Summary *(In one sentence, the main thing God is saying to me through this sermon is . . .)*

_____
_____
_____
_____
_____

Life Application *(The action steps I want to take are . . .)*

_____
_____
_____
_____

My Sermon Notes

Speaker: _____   Text: _____

Date: _____   Topic: _____

_____
_____
_____
_____
_____
_____
_____
_____
_____
_____
_____
_____
_____
_____
_____
_____

Summary *(In one sentence, the main thing God is saying to me through this sermon is . . .)*

_____
_____
_____
_____
_____

Life Application *(The action steps I want to take are . . .)*

_____
_____
_____
_____

extra bible study approach: character study

. . .

Extra Bible Study Approach: Character Study		
Bible Character:		
Date:	Scripture:	Insight:
Summary of insights, key takeaways, and impact on my life:		

Extra Bible Study Approach: Character Study

Bible Character:

Date:	Scripture:	Insight:

Summary of insights, key takeaways, and impact on my life:

Extra Bible Study Approach: Character Study		
Bible Character:		
Date:	Scripture:	Insight:
Summary of insights, key takeaways, and impact on my life:		

extra bible study approach: topic/word study

. . .

Extra Bible Study Approach: Topic/Word Study		
Topic/Word:		
Date:	Scripture:	Insight:
Summary of insights, key takeaways, and impact on my life:		

Extra Bible Study Approach: Topic/Word Study		
Topic/Word:		
Date:	Scripture:	Insight:
Summary of insights, key takeaways, and impact on my life:		

Extra Bible Study Approach: Topic/Word Study		
Topic/Word:		
Date:	Scripture:	Insight:

Summary of insights, key takeaways, and impact on my life:

my prayer journal

. . .

My Prayer Journal

Date: _____

"Lord, what I want to share with You right now is..."

Date: _____

"Lord, what I want to share with You right now is..."

My Prayer Journal

Date: _____

"Lord, what I want to share with You r ght now is…"

Date: _____

"Lord, what I want to share with You r ght now is…"

My Prayer Journal

Date: _____

"Lord, what I want to share with You right now is…"

Date: _____

"Lord, what I want to share with You right now is…"

My Prayer Journal

Date: _____

"Lord, what I want to share with You r ght now is…"

Date: _____

"Lord, what I want to share with You right now is…"

My Prayer Journal

Date: _____

"Lord, what I want to share with You right now is..."

Date: _____

"Lord, what I want to share with You right now is..."

My Prayer Journal

Date: _____

"Lord, what I want to share with You right now is..."

Date: _____

"Lord, what I want to share with You right now is..."

My Prayer Journal

Date: _____

"Lord, what I want to share with You right now is..."

Date: _____

"Lord, what I want to share with You right now is..."

My Prayer Journal

Date: _____

"Lord, what I want to share with You right now is…"

Date: _____

"Lord, what I want to share with You right now is…"

My Prayer Journal

Date: _____

"Lord, what I want to share with You right now is…"

Date: _____

"Lord, what I want to share with You right now is…"

My Prayer Journal

Date: _____

"Lord, what I want to share with You r ght now is…"

Date: _____

"Lord, what I want to share with You r ght now is…"

My Prayer Journal

Date: _____

"Lord, what I want to share with You right now is..."

Date: _____

"Lord, what I want to share with You right now is..."

My Prayer Journal

Date: _____

"Lord, what I want to share with You right now is..."

Date: _____

"Lord, what I want to share with You right now is..."

My Prayer Journal

Date: _____

"Lord, what I want to share with You right now is…"

Date: _____

"Lord, what I want to share with You right now is…"

My Prayer Journal

Date: _____

"Lord, what I want to share with You right now is..."

Date: _____

"Lord, what I want to share with You right now is..."

My Prayer Journal

Date: _____

"Lord, what I want to share with You right now is..."

Date: _____

"Lord, what I want to share with You right now is..."

My Prayer Journal

Date: _____

"Lord, what I want to share with You r ght now is..."

Date: _____

"Lord, what I want to share with You r ght now is..."

My Prayer Journal

Date: _____

"Lord, what I want to share with You right now is..."

Date: _____

"Lord, what I want to share with You right now is..."

my prayer list

. . .

My Prayer List

Request Date: _____   Answer Date: _____

Request:

Answer:

Request Date: _____   Answer Date: _____

Request:

Answer:

Request Date: _____   Answer Date: _____

Request:

Answer:

My Prayer List

Request Date: _____   Answer Date: _____

Request:

Answer:

Request Date: _____   Answer Date: _____

Request:

Answer:

Request Date: _____   Answer Date: _____

Request:

Answer:

My Prayer List

Request Date: _____   Answer Date: _____

Request:

Answer:

Request Date: _____   Answer Date: _____

Request:

Answer:

Request Date: _____   Answer Date: _____

Request:

Answer:

My Prayer List

Request Date: _____   Answer Date: _____

Request:

Answer:

Request Date: _____   Answer Date: _____

Request:

Answer:

Request Date: _____   Answer Date: _____

Request:

Answer:

My Prayer List

Request Date: _____   Answer Date: _____

Request:

Answer:

Request Date: _____   Answer Date: _____

Request:

Answer:

Request Date: _____   Answer Date: _____

Request:

Answer:

My Prayer List

Request Date: _____   Answer Date: _____

Request:

Answer:

Request Date: _____   Answer Date: _____

Request:

Answer:

Request Date: _____   Answer Date: _____

Request:

Answer:

My Prayer List

Request Date: _____   Answer Date: _____

Request:

Answer:

Request Date: _____   Answer Date: _____

Request:

Answer:

Request Date: _____   Answer Date: _____

Request:

Answer:

My Prayer List

Request Date: _____   Answer Date: _____

Request:

Answer:

Request Date: _____   Answer Date: _____

Request:

Answer:

Request Date: _____   Answer Date: _____

Request:

Answer:

My Prayer List

Request Date: _____   Answer Date: _____

Request:

Answer:

Request Date: _____   Answer Date: _____

Request:

Answer:

Request Date: _____   Answer Date: _____

Request:

Answer:

My Prayer List
Request Date: _____   Answer Date: _____   Request: Answer:
Request Date: _____   Answer Date: _____   Request: Answer:
Request Date: _____   Answer Date: _____   Request: Answer:

My Prayer List

Request Date: _____   Answer Date: _____

Request:

Answer:

Request Date: _____   Answer Date: _____

Request:

Answer:

Request Date: _____   Answer Date: _____

Request:

Answer:

My Prayer List

Request Date: _____   Answer Date: _____

Request:

Answer:

Request Date: _____   Answer Date: _____

Request:

Answer:

Request Date: _____   Answer Date: _____

Request:

Answer:

My Prayer List

Request Date: _____   Answer Date: _____

Request:

Answer:

Request Date: _____   Answer Date: _____

Request:

Answer:

Request Date: _____   Answer Date: _____

Request:

Answer:

My Prayer List

Request Date: _____   Answer Date: _____

Request:

Answer:

Request Date: _____   Answer Date: _____

Request:

Answer:

Request Date: _____   Answer Date: _____

Request:

Answer:

My Prayer List

Request Date: _____   Answer Date: _____

Request:

Answer:

Request Date: _____   Answer Date: _____

Request:

Answer:

Request Date: _____   Answer Date: _____

Request:

Answer:

My Prayer List

Request Date: _____   Answer Date: _____

Request:

Answer:

Request Date: _____   Answer Date: _____

Request:

Answer:

Request Date: _____   Answer Date: _____

Request:

Answer:

My Prayer List

Request Date: _____   Answer Date: _____

Request:

Answer:

Request Date: _____   Answer Date: _____

Request:

Answer:

Request Date: _____   Answer Date: _____

Request:

Answer:

my weekly overview

. . .

My Weekly Overview

Week of: _____

Verse of the week:

Daily Time with God:

Mon	Tue	Wed	Thu	Fri	Sat	Sun

Memory Verse:

Prayer Focus:

Bible Reading & Study Goals:

To Do List:

_____ ☐   _____ ☐
_____ ☐   _____ ☐
_____ ☐   _____ ☐
_____ ☐   _____ ☐

Letters/Calls/Emails/Connections:

_____ ☐   _____ ☐
_____ ☐   _____ ☐
_____ ☐   _____ ☐

My Weekly Overview

Week of: _____

Verse of the week:

Daily Time with God:

Mon	Tue	Wed	Thu	Fri	Sat	Sun

Memory Verse:

Prayer Focus:

Bible Reading & Study Goals:

To Do List:

_____ ☐   _____ ☐
_____ ☐   _____ ☐
_____ ☐   _____ ☐
_____ ☐   _____ ☐

Letters/Calls/Emails/Connections:

_____ ☐   _____ ☐
_____ ☐   _____ ☐
_____ ☐   _____ ☐

My Weekly Overview

Week of: _____

Verse of the week:

Daily Time with God:

Mon	Tue	Wed	Thu	Fri	Sat	Sun

Memory Verse:

Prayer Focus:

Bible Reading & Study Goals:

To Do List:

_____ ☐ _____ ☐
_____ ☐ _____ ☐
_____ ☐ _____ ☐
_____ ☐ _____ ☐

Letters/Calls/Emails/Connections:

_____ ☐ _____ ☐
_____ ☐ _____ ☐
_____ ☐ _____ ☐

My Weekly Overview

Week of: _____

Verse of the week:

Daily Time with God:

Mon	Tue	Wed	Thu	Fri	Sat	Sun

Memory Verse:

Prayer Focus:

Bible Reading & Study Goals:

To Do List:

_____ ☐   _____ ☐
_____ ☐   _____ ☐
_____ ☐   _____ ☐
_____ ☐   _____ ☐

Letters/Calls/Emails/Connections:

_____ ☐   _____ ☐
_____ ☐   _____ ☐
_____ ☐   _____ ☐

My Weekly Overview

Week of: _____

Verse of the week:

Daily Time with God:

Mon	Tue	Wed	Thu	Fri	Sat	Sun

Memory Verse:

Prayer Focus:

Bible Reading & Study Goals:

To Do List:

_____ ☐   _____ ☐
_____ ☐   _____ ☐
_____ ☐   _____ ☐
_____ ☐   _____ ☐

Letters/Calls/Emails/Connections:

_____ ☐   _____ ☐
_____ ☐   _____ ☐
_____ ☐   _____ ☐

My Weekly Overview

Week of: _____

Verse of the week:

Daily Time with God:

Mon	Tue	Wed	Thu	Fri	Sat	Sun

Memory Verse:

Prayer Focus:

Bible Reading & Study Goals:

To Do List:

_____ ☐ _____ ☐
_____ ☐ _____ ☐
_____ ☐ _____ ☐
_____ ☐ _____ ☐

Letters/Calls/Emails/Connections:

_____ ☐ _____ ☐
_____ ☐ _____ ☐
_____ ☐ _____ ☐

My Weekly Overview

Week of: _____

Verse of the week:

Daily Time with God:

Mon	Tue	Wed	Thu	Fri	Sat	Sun

Memory Verse:

Prayer Focus:

Bible Reading & Study Goals:

To Do List:

_____ ☐ _____ ☐
_____ ☐ _____ ☐
_____ ☐ _____ ☐
_____ ☐ _____ ☐

Letters/Calls/Emails/Connections:

_____ ☐ _____ ☐
_____ ☐ _____ ☐
_____ ☐ _____ ☐

My Weekly Overview

Week of: _____

Verse of the week:

Daily Time with God:

Mon	Tue	Wed	Thu	Fri	Sat	Sun

Memory Verse:

Prayer Focus:

Bible Reading & Study Goals:

To Do List:

_____ ☐   _____ ☐
_____ ☐   _____ ☐
_____ ☐   _____ ☐
_____ ☐   _____ ☐

Letters/Calls/Emails/Connections:

_____ ☐   _____ ☐
_____ ☐   _____ ☐
_____ ☐   _____ ☐

My Weekly Overview

Week of: _____

Verse of the week:

Daily Time with God:

Mon	Tue	Wed	Thu	Fri	Sat	Sun

Memory Verse:

Prayer Focus:

Bible Reading & Study Goals:

To Do List:

_____ ☐ _____ ☐
_____ ☐ _____ ☐
_____ ☐ _____ ☐
_____ ☐ _____ ☐

Letters/Calls/Emails/Connections:

_____ ☐ _____ ☐
_____ ☐ _____ ☐
_____ ☐ _____ ☐

my spiritual journal

. . .

My Spiritual Journal

Date: _____

Journal Entry:

Date: _____

Journal Entry:

My Spiritual Journal

Date: _____

Journal Entry:

Date: _____

Journal Entry:

My Spiritual Journal

Date: _____

Journal Entry:

Date: _____

Journal Entry:

My Spiritual Journal

Date: _____

Journal Entry:

Date: _____

Journal Entry:

My Spiritual Journal

Date: _____

Journal Entry:

Date: _____

Journal Entry:

My Spiritual Journal

Date: _____

Journal Entry:

Date: _____

Journal Entry:

My Spiritual Journal

Date: _____

Journal Entry:

Date: _____

Journal Entry:

My Spiritual Journal

Date: _____

Journal Entry:

Date: _____

Journal Entry:

My Spiritual Journal

Date: _____

Journal Entry:

Date: _____

Journal Entry:

My Spiritual Journal

Date: _____

Journal Entry:

Date: _____

Journal Entry:

My Spiritual Journal

Date: _____

Journal Entry:

Date: _____

Journal Entry:

My Spiritual Journal

Date: _____

Journal Entry:

Date: _____

Journal Entry:

My Spiritual Journal

Date: _____

Journal Entry:

Date: _____

Journal Entry:

My Spiritual Journal

Date: _____

Journal Entry:

Date: _____

Journal Entry:

My Spiritual Journal

Date: _____

Journal Entry:

Date: _____

Journal Entry:

My Spiritual Journal

Date: _____

Journal Entry:

Date: _____

Journal Entry:

My Spiritual Journal

Date: _____

Journal Entry:

Date: _____

Journal Entry:

My Spiritual Journal

Date: _____

Journal Entry:

Date: _____

Journal Entry:

My Spiritual Journal

Date: _____

Journal Entry:

Date: _____

Journal Entry:

My Spiritual Journal

Date: _____

Journal Entry:

Date: _____

Journal Entry:

My Spiritual Journal

Date: _____

Journal Entry:

Date: _____

Journal Entry:

My Spiritual Journal

Date: _____

Journal Entry:

Date: _____

Journal Entry:

My Spiritual Journal

Date: _____

Journal Entry:

Date: _____

Journal Entry:

My Spiritual Journal

Date: _____

Journal Entry:

Date: _____

Journal Entry:

My Spiritual Journal

Date: _____

Journal Entry:

Date: _____

Journal Entry:

My Spiritual Journal

Date: _____

Journal Entry:

Date: _____

Journal Entry:

My Spiritual Journal

Date: _____

Journal Entry:

Date: _____

Journal Entry:

My Spiritual Journal

Date: _____

Journal Entry:

Date: _____

Journal Entry:

My Spiritual Journal

Date: _____

Journal Entry:

Date: _____

Journal Entry:

My Spiritual Journal

Date: _____

Journal Entry:

Date: _____

Journal Entry:

My Spiritual Journal

Date: _____

Journal Entry:

Date: _____

Journal Entry:

my life-changing experiences

. . .

My Life-Changing Experiences

Date: _____   Location: _____

Life-Changing Experience:

Date: _____   Location: _____

Life-Changing Experience:

My Life-Changing Experiences

Date: _____   Location: _____

Life-Changing Experience:

Date: _____   Location: _____

Life-Changing Experience:

My Life-Changing Experiences

Date: _____   Location: _____

Life-Changing Experience:

Date: _____   Location: _____

Life-Changing Experience:

My Life-Changing Experiences

Date: _____   Location: _____

Life-Changing Experience:

Date: _____   Location: _____

Life-Changing Experience:

My Life-Changing Experiences

Date: _____   Location: _____

Life-Changing Experience:

Date: _____   Location: _____

Life-Changing Experience:

My Life-Changing Experiences

Date: _____   Location: _____

Life-Changing Experience:

Date: _____   Location: _____

Life-Changing Experience:

My Life-Changing Experiences

Date: _____   Location: _____

Life-Changing Experience:

Date: _____   Location: _____

Life-Changing Experience:

My Life-Changing Experiences

Date: _____   Location: _____

Life-Changing Experience:

Date: _____   Location: _____

Life-Changing Experience:

My Life-Changing Experiences

Date: _____   Location: _____

Life-Changing Experience:

Date: _____   Location: _____

Life-Changing Experience:

my ministry of
encouragment

. . .

My Ministry of Encouragement		
Name	Type of Encouragement	Date

My Ministry of Encouragement		
Name	Type of Encouragement	Date

My Ministry of Encouragement		
Name	Type of Encouragement	Date

My Ministry of Encouragement		
Name	Type of Encouragement	Date

My Ministry of Encouragement		
Name	Type of Encouragement	Date

my baton passing
relationships

. . .

My Baton Passing Relationships

Name:
Address:
Phone:
Email: Social Media:
Important Dates (birthday, anniversary, etc.)
Date began meeting:
Areas of initial need:
Scriptures or spiritual growth materials used or given:
Observations:
Spiritual progress:
Date she or he began mentoring another:
Further contact or follow-up:

My Baton Passing Relationships

Name:	
Address:	
Phone:	
Email:	*Social Media:*

Important Dates (birthday, anniversary, etc.)

Date began meeting:

Areas of initial need:

Scriptures or spiritual growth materials used or given:

Observations:

Spiritual progress:

Date she or he began mentoring another:

Further contact or follow-up:

My Baton Passing Relationships
Name:
Address:
Phone:
Email: Social Media:
Important Dates (birthday, anniversary, etc.)
Date began meeting:
Areas of initial need:
Scriptures or spiritual growth materials used or given:
Observations:
Spiritual progress:
Date she or he began mentoring another:
Further contact or follow-up:

My Baton Passing Relationships

Name:
Address:
Phone:
Email: *Social Media:*
Important Dates (birthday, anniversary, etc.)
Date began meeting:
Areas of initial need:
Scriptures or spiritual growth materials used or given:
Observations:
Spiritual progress:
Date she or he began mentoring another:
Further contact or follow-up:

My Baton Passing Relationships
Name:
Address:
Phone:
Email: Social Media:
Important Dates (birthday, anniversary, etc.)
Date began meeting:
Areas of initial need:
Scriptures or spiritual growth materials used or given:
Observations:
Spiritual progress:
Date she or he began mentoring another:
Further contact or follow-up:

my multiplying
movements

. . .

	My Multiplying Movements
Date Completed	*Phases To Launch My Multiplying Movements Group*
	1. Complete *Multiplying Movements* myself.
	2. Practice seeing, stopping, and spending time with people.
	3. List and pray for people God might want me to take through *Multiplying Movements*.
	4. Ask them to consider/pray about meeting together.
	5. Confirm where and when we will meet.
	6. Keep praying and remind group of meeting details.
	7. Launch my group and connect with Forge for support.
	8. As you near the end, encourage your members to launch and begin their own *Multiplying Movements* groups!
Date	*People God may want me to take through Multiplying Movements:*
Date	*People I am intentionally praying for and sharing Jesus with:*

My Multiplying Movements	
Date Completed	*Phases To Launch My Multiplying Movements Group*
	1. Complete *Multiplying Movements* myself.
	2. Practice seeing, stopping, and spending time with people.
	3. List and pray for people God might want me to take through *Multiplying Movements*.
	4. Ask them to consider/pray about meeting together.
	5. Confirm where and when we will meet.
	6. Keep praying and remind group of meeting details.
	7. Launch my group and connect with Forge for support.
	8. As you near the end, encourage your members to launch and begin their own *Multiplying Movements* groups!
Date	*People God may want me to take through Multiplying Movements:*
Date	*People I am intentionally praying for and sharing Jesus with:*

	My Multiplying Movements
Date Completed	*Phases To Launch My Multiplying Movements Group*
	1. Complete *Multiplying Movements* myself.
	2. Practice seeing, stopping, and spending time with people.
	3. List and pray for people God might want me to take through *Multiplying Movements.*
	4. Ask them to consider/pray about meeting together.
	5. Confirm where and when we will meet.
	6. Keep praying and remind group of meeting details.
	7. Launch my group and connect with Forge for support.
	8. As you near the end, encourage your members to launch and begin their own *Multiplying Movements* groups!
Date	*People God may want me to take through Multiplying Movements:*
Date	*People I am intentionally praying for and sharing Jesus with:*

my financial giving

. . .

My Financial Giving

Date:	Income: $	
	Local Church	$
	Missions & Outreach	$
		$
		$
		$
	TOTAL Given	$

Blessings/Notes:

Date:	Income: $	
	Local Church	$
	Missions & Outreach	$
		$
		$
		$
	TOTAL Given	$

Blessings/Notes:

My Financial Giving	
Date:	*Income: $*
Local Church	$
Missions & Outreach	$
	$
	$
	$
TOTAL Given	$

Blessings/Notes:

Date:	*Income: $*
Local Church	$
Missions & Outreach	$
	$
	$
	$
TOTAL Given	$

Blessings/Notes:

My Financial Giving

Date:	Income: $	
	Local Church	$
	Missions & Outreach	$
		$
		$
		$
	TOTAL Given	$

Blessings/Notes:

Date:	Income: $	
	Local Church	$
	Missions & Outreach	$
		$
		$
		$
	TOTAL Given	$

Blessings/Notes:

My Financial Giving	
Date:	*Income: $*
Local Church	$
Missions & Outreach	$
	$
	$
	$
TOTAL Given	$

Blessings/Notes:

Date:	*Income: $*
Local Church	$
Missions & Outreach	$
	$
	$
	$
TOTAL Given	$

Blessings/Notes:

My Financial Giving	
Date:	*Income: $*
Local Church	$
Missions & Outreach	$
	$
	$
	$
TOTAL Given	$

Blessings/Notes:

Date:	*Income: $*
Local Church	$
Missions & Outreach	$
	$
	$
	$
TOTAL Given	$

Blessings/Notes:

my recommended reading

. . .

My Recommended Reading / Books

Title	Author	Date Started	Date Finished

NEED MORE BLANK SPIRITUAL LIFE NOTEBOOK JOURNAL PAGES?

You can print more as needed when these are full, or purchase a bound, blank *Spiritual Life Notebook.*

To purchase, visit ForgeForward.org / resources.

To print, capture the QR Code below to access the Spiritual Life Notebook resource page or go to: www.ForgeForward.org/SLN.

more forge resources

FORGE SPEAKERS & EVENTS
ForgeSpeakers.com
Need someone to challenge your group to become passionate
followers of Jesus who live with hearts on fire and lives on purpose?
Book a Forge speaker for your next event!

FORGE EQUIPPING PROGRAMS for ALL AGES
ForgeTraining.org
Forge Equipping is not summer camp and training events "as usual."
Forge challenges and equips people of all ages to become unique, life-
long Kingdom laborers in their everyday places.

FORGE BOOKS & RESOURCES
ForgeResources.org
Looking for a deeper relationship with God and practical ways to
widen His Kingdom impact through your life? Forge has the resources
you need.

SUBSCRIBE TO FORGE
Get the latest Forge news, weekly devotionals, and prayer updates all year long to encourage you every day, everywhere:
ForgeSubscribe.org

THE FORGE APP
Essential Kingdom laboring tools right at your fingertips:
TheForgeApp.org

JOIN THE MULTIPLYING MOVEMENT
Where everyday followers become Kingdom multipliers:
MultiplyingMovements.com

FORGE VIDEO CONTENT
Subscribe to free video content:
Youtube.com/ForgeForward

FORGE PODCAST
FuelForTheHarvest.com

FORGE DAILY TEXTS
Scan the QR code or visit ForgeForward.org/Sparks
to join Spark of the Day
for one-sentence daily devotionals.

NEED PRAYER?
Email us at Prayer@ForgeForward.org.

CONTACT US
Forge
14485 E. Evans Ave.
Denver, Colorado 80014
303.745.8191 | info@forgefoward.org

scriptures for memorization

Beginning Walk

Hebrews 1:3	Mark 12:30
Hebrews 4:15-16	James 1:12
1 John 1:9	1 Corinthians 10:13

Mark 12:30 (CSB) Love the Lord your God with all your heart, with all your soul, with all your mind, and with all your strength.	**Hebrews 1:3 (CSB)** The Son is the radiance of God's glory and the exact expression of His nature, sustaining all things by His powerful word. After making purification for sins, He sat down at the right hand of the Majesty on high.
James 1:12 (CSB) Blessed is the one who endures trials, because when he has stood the test he will receive the crown of life that God has promised to those who love Him.	**Hebrews 4:15-16 (CSB)** For we do not have a high priest who is unable to sympathize with our weaknesses, but one who has been tempted in every way as we are, yet without sin. Therefore, let us approach the throne of grace with boldness, so that we may receive mercy and find grace to help us in time of need.
1 Corinthians 10:13 (CSB) No temptation has come upon you except what is common to humanity. But God is faithful; He will not allow you to be tempted beyond what you are able, but with the temptation He will also provide the way out so that you may be able to bear it.	**1 John 1:9 (CSB)** If we confess our sins, He is faithful and righteous to forgive us our sins and to cleanse us from all unrighteousness.

Walking with God

James 1:5	Philippians 4:8
Philippians 4:6	Proverbs 3:6
Romans 8:28	Psalm 27:1

Philippians 4:8 (CSB) Finally brothers and sisters, whatever is true, whatever is honorable, whatever is just, whatever is pure, whatever is lovely, whatever is commendable—if there is any moral excellence and if there is anything praiseworthy—dwell on these things.	**James 1:5 (CSB)** Now if any of you lacks wisdom, he should ask God—who gives to all generously and ungrudgingly—and it will be given to him.
Proverbs 3:6 (CSB) In all your ways know Him, and He will make your paths straight.	**Philippians 4:6 (CSB)** Don't worry about anything, but in everything, through prayer and petition with thanksgiving, present your requests to God.
Psalm 27:1 (CSB) The Lord is my light and my salvation—whom should I fear? The Lord is the stronghold of my life—whom should I dread?	**Romans 8:28 (CSB)** We know that all things work together for the good of those who love God, who are called according to His purpose.

The Fruit of the Spirit

John 14:26	John 16:13-14
1 Corinthians 2:9-10	Galatians 4:6
Galatians 5:22-23	1 Corinthians 2:4-5

John 16:13-14 (CSB)
When the Spirit of truth comes, He will guide you into all the truth. For He will not speak on His own, but He will speak whatever He hears. He will also declare to you what is to come. He will glorify Me, because He will take from what is Mine and declare it to you.

John 14:26 (CSB)
But the Counselor, the Holy Spirit, whom the Father will send in My name, will teach you all things and remind you of everything I have told you.

Galatians 4:6 (CSB)
And because you are sons, God sent the Spirit of His Son into our hearts, crying, "Abba, Father!"

1 Corinthians 2:9-10 (CSB)
But as it is written, "What no eye has seen, no ear has heard, and no human heart has conceived—God has prepared these things for those who love Him." Now God has revealed these things to us by the Spirit, since the Spirit searches everything, even the depths of God.

1 Corinthians 2:4-5 (CSB)
My speech and my preaching were not with persuasive words of wisdom but with a demonstration of the Spirit's power, so that your faith might not be based on human wisdom but on God's power.

Galatians 5:22-23 (CSB)
But the fruit of the Spirit is love, joy, peace, patience, kindness, goodness, faithfulness, gentleness, and self-control. The law is not against such things.

Life Witness

Matthew 6:19-21	1 Peter 1:15-16
James 1:22 & 25	1 John 4:7-8
Matthew 5:16	Hebrews 3:13

1 Peter 1:15-16 (CSB) But as the One who called you is holy, you also are to be holy in all your conduct; for it is written, "Be holy, because I am holy."	**Matthew 6:19-21 (CSB)** Don't store up for yourselves treasures on earth, where moth and rust destroy and where thieves break in and steal. But store up for yourselves treasures in heaven, where neither moth nor rust destroys, and where thieves don't break in and steal. For where your treasure is, there your heart will be also.
1 John 4:7-8 (CSB) Dear friends, let us love one another, because love is from God, and everyone who loves has been born of God and knows God. The one who does not love does not know God, because God is love.	**James 1:22 & 25 (CSB)** But be doers of the word and not hearers only, deceiving yourselves. But the one who looks intently into the perfect law of freedom and perseveres in it, and is not a forgetful hearer but a doer who works—this person will be blessed in what he does.
Hebrews 3:13 (CSB) But encourage each other daily, while it is still called today, so that none of you is hardened by sin's deception.	**Matthew 5:16 (CSB)** In the same way, let your light shine before others, so that they may see your good works and give glory to your Father in heaven.

www.ingramcontent.com/pod-product-compliance
Lightning Source LLC
Chambersburg PA
CBHW061141120626
46546CB00005B/1878